M000217015

Living on the Border

Esther de Waal lives in Herefordshire, close to the border between England and Wales, the countryside in which she grew up. A sense of place has always been important and, after getting a degree at Cambridge, she became the first research student in the newly founded Department of Local History at Leicester. It was the buildings and the landscape that led her to her monastic interest in the Benedictine, Cistercian, and Celtic traditions. Her main interests now are her garden and her increasing number of grandchildren, but she also finds time to write, to take retreats, and to give talks, with a particular concern for the visual, the poetic, and the religious imagination.

Living on the Border

Reflections on the Experience of Threshold

Esther de Waal

CANTERBURY
PRESS
Norwich

© Esther de Waal

This edition published in 2011 by the
Canterbury Press Norwich
Editorial office
13–17 Long Lane,
London, EC1A 9PN, UK

Canterbury Press is an imprint of
Hymns Ancient & Modern Ltd (a registered charity)
13a Hellesdon Park Road, Norwich,
Norfolk, NR6 5DR, UK

An enlarged edition of *Living on the Border*, first published in
the UK in 2001 in the *Borders* series by the Canterbury Press
Norwich, and in America in 2004 by Morehouse Publishing
under the title, *To Pause at the Threshold*.

www.canterburypress.co.uk

All rights reserved. No part of this publication may be
reproduced, stored in a retrieval system, or transmitted,
in any form or by any means, electronic, mechanical,
photocopying or otherwise, without the prior permission of
the publisher, Canterbury Press.

The Author has asserted her right under the Copyright,
Designs and Patents Act, 1988,
to be identified as the Author of this Work

British Library Cataloguing in Publication data

A catalogue record for this book is available
from the British Library

978 1 85311 962 0

Typeset by Regent Typesetting, London

Contents

For
my grandson
ADAN

Introduction

There is a traditional saying of ancient wisdom: 'A threshold is a sacred thing.' In some places of the world, in some traditional cultures, and in monastic life, this is still remembered. It is something, however, that we often forget today, and I would count myself among those who do not always find it easy to remember. But it is something that I have deliberately been attempting to recover for myself, and which I now want to share. I hope this book encourages others to take time to pause at the threshold.

When I visited Japan I experienced the role of the threshold in a very simple daily experience. Before entering the house, the Japanese will stop in order to remove the shoes worn outside in the street. Upon entering the house, they put on slippers placed inside the door. This forces a very deliberate and conscious way of standing still, even if for only a moment, in order to show respect for the difference between two spaces, the outer and the inner: the preparation for the encounter with another person, another household.

This is very similar to the traditional monastic practice of *statio*, which also pays homage to the threshold moment, and shows reverence for the handling of space and time. The monk or nun enters the church for the saying of the daily offices, but always leaves him- or herself time to stand, to wait, to let go of all the demands of whatever the previous activity had been, with all its concurrent anxieties and expectations. That stillness permits each one to enter into that space kept empty in the heart for the Word of God. By rushing, whether through a sense of duty or obligation, or to save a few extra moments for the task in hand, they may gain something in terms of daily work. What is lost, however, is the attention, the awareness of the crossing over into the time and the place for *opus Dei*, the work of God.

Discovering the traditional practices of the Celtic peoples, as they have come down by word of mouth, has shown me how hard-working and demanding lives can still be shaped by time taken to recognize and to rejoice in the succession of times of change, in each day, in every season, year by year, in the pattern of life itself from birth to death. The Celts had their rituals and their celebrations for acknowledging these times of change, and I have included them in this book, for I myself have gained so much from trying to incorporate them into my own life. But I also feel that there are wider implications here for the way that we address our public lives, in all the inescapable issues in church, in politics, and the world situation.

I have written elsewhere about learning to see with wonder and delight, about mystery, about the amazing universe that opens up for me when I look at a flower or a stone through a magnifying glass.[1] But I want now to take

as my starting point what I have received from the landscape around my home, the countryside where I grew up
and where I have now returned to live, the border country
between England and Wales. At this stage of my life, I am
setting out to uncover – though it might be better to speak
of it as to recover or to rediscover – it in such a way that
the exterior landscape may shape and mould the interior
landscape.

For I am not writing just about a rural situation of
great beauty, with a history stretching far back into time.
In this book I want to read a landscape so that it reveals
itself and gives an image of God at work in his world.
Above all, I want to explore the role of thresholds, of the
crossing-over places, not only geographical ones but also
metaphorical thresholds.

I have found that these same thresholds have been
explored by a writer growing up in totally different circumstances from my own who described how, as a young boy,
he realized the significance of belonging to two worlds.
His growing up in these two worlds sharpened his percep-
tion so that he later saw it as a formative experience. The
twentieth-century English novelist Graham Greene wrote
a travel book in which he gave the subtitle 'Across the
River' to his opening chapter 'The Border'. Yet, in fact,
his journey lay across dry land with neither river nor sea
in the vicinity. And that at once reminds us of the role
of the image and the part that it is bound to play in the
exploration of crossing over, boundaries, thresholds – the
theme I wish to explore in this small book.

All our lives are inevitably made of a succession of
borders and thresholds, which open up into the new,
and promise excitement or fear. The traveller encounter-
ing unknown places has all the exhilaration, the thrill of

another country. Graham Greene writes vividly of the expectancy waiting on the further side:

> Over there everything is going to be different; life is never going to be quite the same again after your passport has been stamped and you find yourself speechless among the money-changers. The man seeking scenery imagines stranger woods and unheard-of mountains; the romantic believes that the women over the border will be more beautiful and complaisant than those at home; the unhappy man imagines at least a different hell; the suicidal traveller expects the death he never finds. The atmosphere of the border – it is like starting over again, there is something about it like a good confession . . .[2]

This passage is about a geographical border between two countries. But from his early childhood Greene knew the juxtaposition of two metaphorical countries, for his home was part of a large boarding school and he had only to open a door to move between two worlds: one smelling of books and fruit and eau de cologne, and the other of damp towels and ink and disinfectant. Sometimes he lived surrounded by a gentle croquet lawn, with flowerbeds and raspberry canes, and at other times by great square buildings of harsh brick, stone stairs, and cracked bells. He was an inhabitant of both countries, sometimes on one side of the door and sometimes on the other. Pulled by these different ties, he asked: 'How can life on a border be other than restless?'

I, too, have lived in more than one world. I have come back to live where I grew up. I have returned to the slower rhythms and the earthlinked textures of life on the

Welsh Borders. Life here is a total contrast to the years spent elsewhere, in a big university in the Midlands or an important cathedral city in the crowded southeast of England. As I root myself here I am finding that it is at once familiar and strange. This landscape has become my teacher, my mentor.

It takes time to recognize this, but I am beginning to realize just how profound an effect it has had on my life, on the way that I approach time, people, situations, and issues. I suppose that I might sum it up by saying that I have become aware of the continual movement of crossing over thresholds into the new, while still of course being part of what is left behind. It applies, above all, in my own life and in the emerging pattern that I discern now that I am (as my journalist son put it so magnificently) on the cusp of old age. But it has also influenced the way in which I look at situations and how I relate to other people. As I try to sum it up, a whole galaxy of words starts to come tumbling out: openness to change, ready and willing to move forward, living without defences rather than hiding behind barriers. In the end, if I were to find one single word that catches this sense of thresholds opening up to what is new and unknown, it would be *transformation* – and transformations, as L. William Countryman reminds us, 'are always at least a little scary'. To be transformed implies letting go of control for a while in the hopeful expectation that something worthwhile may result. It means taking the risk that old certainties might be replaced by a new way of seeing the world. Another word is *conversion*, not in the relatively easy sense of changing to religion, or from one denomination to another, but in the much more demanding sense of 'turning round', and 'discovering that there's a whole world out there that you hadn't really been aware of'.[3]

I can only learn from this border countryside landscape when I let its presence reveal itself to me gently, so that I begin to sense its patterns – those hill rhythms and water rhythms that had such a profound effect upon David Jones, the artist and poet, when he lived a few miles away at Capel-y-ffin in the Llanthony valley in the Black Mountains. In an autobiographical talk he said that in those years between 1924 and 1926, as he came to know the valley and the hills, he found that his work was influenced by the strong hill rhythms and the bright counter-rhythms of the water brooks. He found that there was no stillness in this landscape, but that here the movement of streams, wind, rain, and clouds ceaselessly transformed – in change that reveals the unchanging.[4]

Landscape at Capel-y-ffin by David Jones.

Already I am being brought into a world where significant things are shown as images, and insight comes from shapes and patterns, from the visual rather than from the written word. Here I come face to face with what is elemental, both in my own self and in the world around. So although I began with the experience of a physical landscape, I have been taken beyond that to explore successively the interplay of light and dark, of time and season, as they alternate and move on, and my own life as it also moves forward. I consider how I am to embrace change in the context of the movement from birth to death, with its universal and inescapable stages. Am I willing to cross the threshold of new understanding by being open and receptive, not closed in and defensive? These questions also arise as I think not only about physical growth but also about growth into understanding and wisdom. The most profound threshold, however, remains that between the inner and the outer, between going deeper into the interior self and emerging to meet the world beyond the self without protective defences, as friend not as foe.

How can a life on the border be other than restless, as Graham Greene wrote? That is one of the questions that I want to address. I feel, and I guess I am not alone in this, that more and more of us are finding ourselves in a place where two worlds meet, and I ask, 'How do I hold this together? How do I make this a creative encounter? How do I stop myself from being pulled in one direction or the other?' There seems to be no easy or obvious answer to these questions. But I see that moment of crossing over as the threshold moment, the pause between, and this I believe holds the key to what I hope to explore.

The Border Landscape

Reading a landscape

I am now setting out to uncover or rediscover a whole world that lies around me, and to discover it in such a way that the outer landscape might shape and mould the inner landscape. It is an exploration that I believe I can best undertake by using the imagination in image and poetry and metaphor. As I turn to the land and to its poets and artists, I want to make this an undertaking not only for myself. I hope that my own specific encounter with a specific place may also speak to my readers and give them images that they can relate to their own personal experiences. This book comes out of a particular place that I know, but it is ultimately about making any place or any circumstance the threshold into the other, the new, the strange, and showing the image of difference, mystery, otherness at work in God's world.

Although my earliest childhood was spent in the Welsh

border countryside, I was never taught to read the land-scape around me. I did not ask questions about it, for neither did my father. He was an antiquarian of the old school and I owe him my sense of history and my knowledge of medieval architecture. His approach was quintessentially that of a man fascinated by factual inform-ation of a most precise nature. He wanted to be able to date stones, whether in their natural state or shaped and used by local builders, but these were not living stones: they did not cry out. This was a world on which categories and labels were imposed, a world known through charts and charters, dates and land grants. These land charters, with their concern for the giving and transferring of land between one owner and another, between one estate and another, encouraged an attitude of certainty and clarity about the past.

From my mother I learned another sort of certainty: certainty about the present, for she held very clear ideas about our neighbours across the border in Wales. Prej-udice simplified her approach: the Welsh were small in stature, unreliable in character, not to be trusted, and unworthy of any respect. 'Taffy was a Welshman, Taffy was a thief', the old jingle tripped only too easily off the tongue. They came to raid, crossing over into England to make inroads into our fair and pleasant land. There-fore, there was not any idea of giving and receiving, and doorways were shut, defrauding me of what, even as a small child, might have taught me to be receptive, ready to learn from the other. I had no sense of thresholds to cross, or borders to break; there was nothing to encour-age openness or exploration.

Living on the border

But as so often happens in life, I was given a second chance. When I was married and with four young sons, my father presented us with a small cottage – two rooms upstairs and two rooms downstairs, the traditional local pattern, with only one cold water tap and no inside lavatory. Two streams meet here, the Cwm and the Greidol, and flow over into a waterfall, where at the base lies a mass of huge rock slabs whose shape and position would gradually but dramatically change over the years under the impact of flood and storm. These swirling combinations of mud and silt and stone, continually different and new, gave me a metaphor for a natural configuration that maintains its essential form while retaining its ability to shape and adapt over the years. Since time immemorial, streams have formed the boundaries between properties and settlements and very often, as here, they still carry their earliest Celtic or Welsh names. But even though the streams' names might be Welsh, the village name was Saxon and politically part of England, even while the church is still the proud possessor of the Great Welsh Bible, the first Bible to be translated into Welsh by William Morgan in 1588. A mile or two away, the neighbouring tiny church of Llangua – which can date its origins to a sixth-century Celtic saint – lies geographically in Wales while yet remaining in the Church of England. Any neat demarcation, whether religious, economic, or cultural, has little meaning in a border countryside such as this.

So when I went walking along the stretch of Offa's Dyke that ran only a few miles away, I came to know afresh the world that had earlier delighted my father. He had told me the heroic story of Offa and his eighth-century ambitions, the man who dominated the whole of Britain between 757 and 795, a contemporary and almost an equal of the emperor Charlemagne. But that was now something of the historic past. A military frontier had become a pastoral border, though with visible differences whose pattern one could see written on the land itself. It was still a place where two worlds met. I felt that I was looking beyond political ambition and military conquest. Of course I could see those differences: they were written into the pattern of the landscape. There was Wales on the west side, a country of mountains and scattered settlements, bare stretches of hillside covered with sheep and wild ponies. I recalled David Jones's delight in the legend that these were the descendants of the horses of Arthur's knights, when they ran free after the defeat of the king and the end of Arthurian Britain. Now shrunk in size 'those straying riderless horses gone to grass in forest and on mountain, seem, as their masters, to have acquired a new yet aboriginal liberty'.[1] On the east side, in contrast, lay a rolling landscape of low hills and prosperous farms where neat hedgerows enclosed fields that were the result of the more fertile soil and the strength of the landowning families. Two different worlds met here, each with its own past, shaped by geography, politics, and people.

Through others' eyes

So as I live here once again I am presented by the simple reality of the land. It is my mentor, my teacher, and in it I have a guide who can never become theoretical or abstract, for I am learning the wisdom of the earth itself, the ground beneath my feet, the people who settled it and shaped its cultivation. Above all, living deep in the countryside, I am faced with what I could so easily be unaware of in a city: the alternation of light and dark, the changing patterns of the seasons and the years, the ebb and flow of solstice and equinox.

As I return to live here, I find a place, a situation, that is both familiar and mysterious. That is right. It should take time for something to reveal itself, to unveil its meaning. Many of us were struck by the way in which, when he was asked a question during a radio interview, Archbishop Rowan Williams said, 'May I take a moment?' For many of us who were listening, accustomed as we had become to the cut and thrust of the quick question and the immediate response in public discussion, this was a defining moment. It reminded us just how important it is to pause, in this as in any other context. It is to recall the role of reverence and respect, in a question, in another person, in a situation.

This is what I have gained from my encounter with my native landscape. In the end, this border country and what it brings must remain elusive, like the mists and the ever-changing colours. It will speak to each of us differently, and it will say different things to us at different times. It will strike chords and bring glimpses. It may also bring gifts of sudden insight. But it can never be possessed or fully understood. All of this is a reason for great gratitude.

The landscape, as David Jones reminds me, also points me to an awareness of movement, change, and ceaseless transformation. If I were to try to sum it up very simply, I would say that it has made me aware of continual movement, crossing over thresholds while yet remaining

firmly rooted in this place where I still belong. So at once
I realize that I am in a situation that is not sheltered and
safe, for to be transformed means being open, and while
standing firmly in this place where I belong, I am firmly
rooted yet never static.

R. S. Thomas, the Welsh poet *par excellence* of our
day, is also, in effect, speaking of the importance of being
hesitant at the threshold, when he holds out this warning
to those who have become too possessive of what they see
of his native country:

> You can come in
> You can come a long way . . .
> But you won't be inside.[2]

This encounter with place is such a personal experience that it is not surprising to find that the one thing all
writers, whether of prose or poetry, have in common is
that they respect the way in which landscape opens up
depths beyond itself. Bonnie Thurston, an American poet
and theologian who has come to know and love the Welsh
Borders, brings her own particular vision of the land:

> On a glorious summer day
> this border country rolls out
> in a carpet of green turf,
> the fertile result
> of a blood-soaked history.
> A place where armies marched,
> kings were made and broken . . .
>
> Border lands often murmur
> of what was and might have been . . .

God draws back the veil
to make a Golden Valley
between the Black Mountains,
a place teeming with the life of
presence and past.[3]

There is great gentleness and hope in these lines. The past
is there with its memories of battle and death, and there
is blood-soaked land, but there is also fertility, the green
turf that has sprung from the destruction. Above all there
is the Golden Valley with all the promise that its name
inspires. As God draws back the veil we see how this
landscape sings. Here is the good news: different cultures
and stories meet and mix, they challenge one another,
and from their meeting the new can flourish.

Border or frontier?

By a strange irony there is a place I visit frequently and with
which I have a strong connection that allows me to meas-
ure the strength of and appreciate the gift that I receive
at home more fully. As I was thinking about the theme
of this small book, I spent three months in a Benedictine
monastery in South Africa, uMariya uMama weThemba,
founded by the American Episcopalian Order of the Holy
Cross. This became particularly significant, for I found
that I was now beginning to ask myself questions: What
is a frontier? A border? A boundary? A threshold?

A boundary gives a necessary definition – a structure,
a framework that one respects. The whole monastic life
shows us the vital role of that – boundaries of time and
place, held in a flexible rhythm that brings order and

certainty, and with this comes freedom (as it does of course in the parallel situation of the family).[4] Boundaries, any good psychologist will tell us (and the monastic tradition has an excellent grasp of psychological insight), are very important and must be respected. A frontier, however, is designed to exclude the other. It is the product of hostility, aggression, and power. But my experience is of the Welsh Marches, neither boundary nor frontier, but a borderland that marks (where of course the old term Marches or Marcher Lords originates) the point where the lands of two peoples run alongside one another. So I see borderlands as places where different cultures and histories meet and mix, perhaps challenge one another, and from which the new can then open up. And what I find in this outer landscape (which is my home) has also become true of that inner landscape, the inscape, which I cultivate and nurture.

In the eastern Cape in South Africa, I was able to see a complete contrast in the way an imperial power had established frontiers to keep peoples apart. In order to push the Xhosa people back beyond the great Fish River, the British created a network of fortified positions along a line marked by palisades and forts, manned by constant patrols intended to maintain 'a proper degree of terror'. Here was a deliberate policy of creating barriers in order to establish a clear demarcation line between cultural and racial difference, white and black, by excluding and dividing. First written, as it were, on the soil itself in the nineteenth century, it was next to be carried over into legal, social, and economic spheres in the twentieth century under the regime of apartheid. The white proponents of that regime were so completely and utterly confident of the rightness of their stance that they shut the door totally on the other. Metaphorically, they barricaded themselves into their *laagers*, those circles of upturned wagons that the Afrikaners traditionally used to protect themselves on their long marches. Two worlds had now become polarized, without contact, without sympathy or understanding.

A border priory

In the Welsh Marches I realized with gratitude that I belonged to a world where both landscape and buildings gave me another message. St Mary's Priory in Monmouth, a few miles from my home, is a border place in every sense. It tells a wonderful story of how cultures and peoples have met and mingled there. We find a Benedictine priory built in Wales after the Norman Conquest, a daughter house founded from a mother house in the Loire Valley in France, but also having a Breton involvement, which introduces a Celtic element. In the preface to the history of the priory church, Rowan Williams, then the Archbishop of Wales and bishop of Monmouth, explores the full significance of such a border situation:

This history gives us a good metaphor for a central aspect of Christian ministry. The priory built on a past legacy but moved in a new direction; it was founded by strangers who were also kindred. It is a 'border' place in every sense; and the future of the priory buildings must be about how that border is explored in such a way as to change strangers into kindred, and to bring people closer to that dangerous and transforming border between the world and God – the border that God himself upsets by his entry into the world on our terms, in flesh and blood.

Across the border, then, whether it's a human border or the strange frontier with God, is something or someone who is more hospitable than we dreamed; and we learn this by taking the risk of hospitality ourselves. Benedictine life is centred on God and on guests, seeing each in the other and learning from each how to relate to the other.[5]

Interlude: Standing on the Threshold

Threshold stone at Hereford Cathedral by Richard Kindersley.

Rowan Williams tells us to take the risk of hospitality. When we turn to the Rule of St Benedict, we are shown the fullness of what hospitality can mean. It is not merely the open door or the open gate that offers warmth, food, and drink, but also the open heart offering acceptance and love, and not least the open mind ready and willing to listen and to receive and exchange. St Benedict tells us to give a welcome to all who come because we see in them the figure of Christ himself. This means not judging or labelling, not being critical or competitive, not imprisoning the other in our demands and expectations. As he so often does, St Benedict presents profound theological teaching in very down-to-earth and immediate terms. In Chapter 62 he describes the porter who stands at the gate of the monastery to exercise this art of hospitality on behalf of his brothers.

It is tender, funny, and wise, a very simple but profound portrait, and we should not overlook its implications as a model for any of us. We see a man on the threshold, with one foot, as it were, in the monastic enclosure and the other in the world outside. Whenever anyone appears, he calls out his greeting '*Deo Gratias*': 'Thank God you have come.' It is a real welcome, of loving openness, and St Benedict uses two very simple phrases to describe it: 'all the gentleness that comes from the fear of God' and 'the warmth of love'.

In my own thinking and praying I have extended the image of the man on the margin to include the greeting of new circumstances, new situations, and new demands, so that even when they appear unexpectedly and I feel unready and ill equipped, I am yet prepared to welcome them. This image of being simultaneously rooted yet open, planted on either side of the threshold of the interior and the exterior, is one that I now want to apply elsewhere in my own personal experience.

2

Times and Seasons: Crossing
Between Light and Dark

Place and time are the two primordial, inescapable realities that can either imprison or liberate us. How do we handle them? Even recognizing this and realizing that it is our responsibility can be the first step to freedom. I find that I have been given an unexpected image in the form of the medieval chained library of Hereford Cathedral, and as the priest–poet David Scott reminds us, if we are thinking of heaven and earth – 'two major and distinct realities and you want to build some sort of bridge between them' – then we can only deal in images that have always been tools for writers for the exploration of truths.[1] In Hereford Cathedral we find the Mappa Mundi, which is not actually a map in the usual sense but instead, in an apparently geographical map, gives us a picture of the medieval understanding of the world. Jerusalem is placed at the centre, surrounded by countries and creatures, true or fantastical, which make up a total universe, real and imaginary, human and non-human; and in the triangular apex above the round world is Christ in Majesty presiding over it all, the work of his creation and redemption. We see God seated in glory and in judgment, inside and outside of time. And so here I am given an image of another border: that between time and eternity.[2]

For many of us, time has become yet one more commodity of the consumer world, a commodity at the mercy of the dictates of deadlines and contracts, valued in terms of achievement and productivity. It is not easy to regain a sense of the changes of time and season when the night sky with all its gentle and subtle changes is blotted out by the sullen orange glow of the sodium light, denying us what should rightly be the timeless heritage of the movement of moon and stars. When the imported luxuries of the world stare us in the face on every visit to the supermarket, we are denied any sense of the coming and going of successive seasons of the year, with the expectation and delight that each will bring its own particular gift. If the kiwi fruits and the tomatoes and the strawberries are endlessly available, there is no longer that waiting on the threshold for each new season to bring its appropriate contribution of fruitfulness.

Yet living here I cannot fail to be aware of movement, the movement of water, of light and dark, of the coming and going of each season in turn, and with it the underlying theme of ebb and flow, of death and life, the dying down of nature and the new seed of creation and re-creation, experienced again and again, year in year out, just as it will be repeated time and again throughout our lives. It demands active response, involvement. I remember hearing that Parker Palmer was once told about what to expect from an upper mid-west winter: 'The winters will drive you crazy until you learn to get out into them.'

In an attempt to remember, to recall, to live with these as gifts, to handle light and dark, time and season with respect and reverence, I have begun in recent years to look at the annual pattern of the changeover of the days and the seasons as the Celtic peoples of the Scottish islands used to do. I have made a commitment to incorporate into my own life the riches of the Celtic oral tradition that has come down to us from generation to generation and shows us so vividly their way of looking at the world. Of course in my case it applies very easily since I also live in a northern clime, but it is the underlying approach and attitude that I want to encourage people to discover and use for themselves, in their own terms.

Every day each of us experiences that alternation between night and day as we move between dawn and dusk, between being asleep and awake. After all, life is shaped by this regular border movement written into daily life in an inescapable pattern of crossing over between the two. Both the light and the dark have always captured the imagination of writers and poets, of theologians, of all early peoples living close to the land. When I came upon these words from a Christmas sermon by St Leo the Great, the fifth-century pope, I wondered, as I have wondered so often, why we neglect the riches of our great Christian tradition, and as a result do not use the glorious energy in a passage such as this:

O man [and woman] rouse yourself!
Learn to know the dignity of your nature.
. . .
Use this visible creation as it should be used,

as you use the earth, sea, sky, air, springs and rivers;
and whatever is beautiful and wonderful
in them acknowledging the praise and glory of God.
Touch the physical light with the bodily sense
and embrace with all the power of your soul
that true light . . .[3]

Naturally the coming of the light had practical conse-
quences that inspired the daily rituals we find among the
Celtic peoples, since the coming of morning light, and the
cessation of that light each night, governed their life and
work. It is important that, as we read these prayers and
blessings today, we put them into the context of gaining
a livelihood in circumstances that were harsh, unroman-
tic, and unsafe, a world that demanded courage. Ritual
brought a sense of order into what they did, and connected them with the reality of time and season.

The pattern of the day

Living on the borders brings me a very clear sense of the
movement of time – of light and dark, of the changing
seasons – and with it the underlying themes of death and
life, darkness and light, creation and re-creation, inescapable for any of us whether we live in an urban or a
rural environment. For here we find ourselves touched
by something primal, that repetition of birth and death,
dying and new life, experienced again and again, year in
and year out, repeated throughout our lives.

The Celtic world had rituals for every day and every
season, so the passage of time was marked with due reverence and awareness. The day would start by saluting

the rising sun, whom they hailed as they would a great person returning to their land. When the sun rose over the tops of the peaks, an old man in Arisaig would remove his headcovering and bow his head down, giving glory to the great God of life for the magnificence of the sun and for the goodness of its light to the children of men and to the animals of the world.

> Hail to thee, thou sun of the seasons,
> As thou traversest the skies aloft,
> Thy steps are strong on the wing of the heavens.[4]

Inside the house the woman lays the foundation of her domestic duties by spreading the embers of the fire, which has been burning throughout the night, in three equal sections in a circle, putting a peat between them so that each will touch the small boss in the middle that forms the common centre. The first peat is laid down in the name of the God of Life, the second in the name of the God of Peace, the third in the name of the God of Grace, and the circle is then covered in the name of the Three of Light. Fire, light, warmth – the image of the nurturing and sustaining hand of God and of the need for these same qualities within our own selves, is here enacted as a daily ritual. This custom can easily seem romantic and distant, far removed from the technology of the electric switch, the automatic coffee maker, the electric kettle, or whatever forms the first ritual of bringing warmth into the start of our day. And yet the reality of performing an action with awareness, consciousness of the presence of God, gratitude for his gifts of power or water or light, still remains the same. An action undertaken consciously and with reverence gives meaning to the start of the day and thus to a hallowing of time and its handling with care.

In the Celtic tradition, this daily celebration of the coming of the light of each day then became a daily reminder of heaven, of the future light of eternity:

> O God, who broughtest me from the rest of last night
> Unto the joyous light of this day,
> Be Thou bringing me from the new light of this day
> Unto the guiding light of eternity.
> Oh! from the new light of this day
> Unto the guiding light of eternity.

Then there is a prayer in the evening, as the light fades at dusk, at the time of 'the change-over routine', as naturalists in Africa call that moment when evening falls and the wild creatures welcome the coming of the darkness.

> I am in hope, in its proper time,
> That the great and gracious God
> Will not put out for me the light of grace
> Even as thou dost leave me this night.

This is a reminder of something that is only too easy to forget in a culture of urban values: both the light and the dark have a role to play. John Davies, a bishop who has known both Africa and England, and who now lives on the borders in North Wales, reminds us: 'There is a place within the providence of God for the darkness, the night, the shadow. Our individual formation is in the dark, between conception and birth. The mysterious workings of our bodies are in the dark. The seed grows secretly in the dark . . . We need to recognise and work with this darkness, even when we feel that it is opposing the light which is the primary gift of God.'[5]

'Darkness and light are both alike to Thee,' sings the

psalmist, and just as we can learn so much from the songs
of the people of Israel, so we also learn from the songs
that were always in the hearts and on the lips of the Celtic
peoples. They make me conscious of what otherwise I
might easily neglect, those crossing-over moments that
carry me between the dark and the light, the light and the
dark, taking me daily and yearly from one to the other.

> The eye of the great God
> The eye of the God of glory,
> The eye of the King of hosts,
> The eye of the King of the living,
> Pouring upon us
> At each time and season
> Pouring upon us
> Gently and generously.

There are so many prayers throughout the ages on the
celebration of the coming of the light – the light that is
the dawn, that is the light of life, that is Christ himself. I
end this section with one that I have taken from Bede, so
that if we turn to the Celtic tradition we do not forget the
riches of the Anglo-Saxon world:

> Grant us your light, O Lord,
> that the darkness in our hearts
> being wholly passed away,
> we may come at last to the light
> which is Christ.
> For Christ is the morning star,
> who when the night of this world has passed,
> brings to us
> the promised light of life,
> and opens to them eternal day. Amen.[6]

Praying the seasons

In recent years I have begun quite consciously to live the pattern of time in the Celtic way and it has given me much joy because now I value change as I never did before. What I most appreciate is that four times in each year there is a pause, a festival, a named day, marking the transitional moment between one season and the next. For as the sun annually passed through its four stations, the equinoxes and the solstices became significant moments of the year. They were celebrated as a succession of threshold moments, each with its name and its rituals to carry men and women forward to the next season.

The year began at Samhaine on 1 November. Country folk around me still speak of this as 'the turning of the year', and for many people, whether they celebrate the pre-Christian Samhaine or the Christian feasts of All Saints and All Souls, this is the thinnest time of the year, the time at which the veil between time and eternity can easily become transparent. With the drawing in of the days, the coming of darkness, and the prospect of winter with all its attendant hardships and ills, this was the time to bring the flocks down from their summer pastures, and those animals that could not be kept would be slaughtered and their carcasses and bones burnt in bonfires. In the words of the twentieth-century poet of the Hebrides George Mackay Brown, it was as if 'the children of the sun were entreating the light to return from darkness, to stay with them, to provide them with corn and milk and fleeces through the lessening days of autumn and winter'.[7] The landscape becomes bare, stripped, cold, stark, dead.

Can we still find significance in the passing of the seasons? Can we live into them in such a way that we allow their changes to shape the pattern of our prayer? It is undoubtedly easier in a place where I can watch the moon wax and wane, see the stars move across the horizon, see the trees gain and lose their foliage, and notice the gradual shading of the colours around me. To begin the year with the drawing in of the days from 1 November, which I have now begun to do, has become significant and powerful in my own life. It must inevitably take a different form in a town, but if you look you can still try to find the images that encourage turning the cycle of the seasons into reflective praying.

Fr Philip Jebb OSB, former Prior of the Benedictine Abbey of Downside, has given us his own response:

Winter has a message all its own;
. . .
The trees are naked, without leaves or flowers or fruit;
But the bare branches give us glimpses of the stars;
They reach their fingers to heaven,
Even as their roots hold fast to the earth.
Linked by the strong trunk, giving interchange of life,
symbols of our dual nature and inheritance.[8]

Spring comes with the feast of Imbolc on 1 February (which is also the feast of St Brigid, and the following day is Candlemas). This is the time of the lactation of the ewes, and for those of us in the northern hemisphere, the moment when the first shoots of new growth start to break through the dark soil, drawn by the promise of sunlight.

We breathe a new air,
No longer cold with seeming death.

The flowers respond
to the strengthening Sun, your light.
So may our hearts respond to your love and grace.
The birds break into song and call us to your praise.
So may our hearts give praise at all aspects of our
    lives.
The frozen earth and water melt to new life:
So may our hardened hearts be softened
to gentleness and love.
We are overwhelmed with images, symbols,
confirmations of your resurrecting, your enlivening.

The year is swinging on its pivot and bringing us to the start
of summer, celebrated on 1 May as the feast of Beltaine.
Now that the light begins to overtake the dark, the days
lengthen and nights are shorter. It was the time when the
flocks would be taken from their winter quarters to graze
and fatten in the high meadows throughout the summer.
The people moved with their animals so that there was
a regular transition. The farm names *hendre* and *hafod*,
found throughout the area, refer to these winter and summer farms respectively, so that the landscape still carries
a reminder of the yearly pattern of transition.

If Imbolc is the season of light, Beltaine is the season of
growth, and prayer becomes praise for fulfilment:

Strong image of your creative power,
Calling forth the endless variety of your creative
Imagination:
Colour, scent and sound.
Making for Beauty
And for peaceful Joy.

Finally, on 1 August the feast of Lammas marks the beginning of the harvest when the earth brings its fruits to birth. Because of the new pattern of the year dictated to us by school terms and holidays, which cut across the older and more natural rhythms of the seasons, the common assumption is to regard August as the height of summer, the time for seaside vacations, camping, journeys abroad. But I have found that to follow the Celtic sense of timing now feels much more convincing. For this is harvest time, the gathering in of the fruits, the time to celebrate the main subsistence crops, whether of the fields, the hedgerows, or the orchards – and not least the time for their storing, conserving, and preserving in whatever way is the most appropriate to each. Sadly, for many today, this process is disappearing, for the speed at which we live and the ease of frozen food have meant the loss of those earlier traditional skills that respected the unique character and quality of each thing as it came to ripen and be gathered and handled accordingly.

The Orthodox liturgy of the Transfiguration on 6 August ends with the blessing of the first fruits. This should be one of the most joyous times because the threshold of plenty has been crossed. So Philip Jebb prays:

The flowers have turned to seeds and fruit,
For our enjoyment,
Our sustenance,
And our future life.
This is the time of fulfilment and completion.
It had a beauty of its own:
Perfect symbol of your providence.
We rejoice in the fruits you give us
in your loving generosity.

3

Embracing Life's Changes

From birth to death

Can this theme of crossing the borders apply to the pattern of my own life? What about all those transitions that occur from birth to death? They are not generally marked by ritual apart from the three events for which today's society has fashionable social (and religious) gatherings: baptism, marriage, and death. Christenings, weddings, and funerals are ceremonies that reflect important public high moments, and this is absolutely right. But they do not help when I feel the need for something in addition, for some ritual that will recognize that in all our lives there is a succession of passing-over moments, many of which must remain secret and private.

The traditional worldview, entrenched into every African child's psyche, speaks of inter-related worlds, the world of the living and the world of the dead, together making one whole and complete community under God's

LIVING ON THE BORDER

direct control and influence. African people belong to these two worlds that overlap and inter-connect. They never forget the spirit world, the human being as part of a bigger system. They see Earth as a gift from God, the rendezvous of the dead and the living. They speak to us of what is fundamental, universal, and what all of us recognize as being part of that primal vision – to which we are heir – even though sometimes we have neglected it, and with God's grace need to reclaim.

In the *Carmina Gadelica* we see how, until quite recently, life in the Scottish highlands and islands had its rituals and blessings for every stage of the life of the household. Family members conducted the rituals in the home itself. From the moment of birth, the mother would make a distinction between the more formal clerical, or 'great', baptism in church and the birth baptism over which she presided in the house. The newborn child would be passed three times across the hearth and then carried three times sunwise (the pattern of the sun's daily journey) around the hearth, ensuring its insertion into the natural rhythm and flow of the universe, and then finally three drops of water would be placed on the baby's head. Here are timeless, primal elements, powerful images that transcend our immediate experience.

Coming of age

I was reminded of just how powerful such rituals can, and perhaps should, be from my experience of Africa. In Zimbabwe, or Rhodesia as it was then, the ears of the young boys were pierced as the first step of initiation into manhood. A doctor whose family has long belonged there and who understands this rite tells us that this 'opened' his ear to things of the spirit, and enabled him to listen properly to worldly matters and understand them, to listen with understanding more than just as a child. This is all part of that African sense of progress into knowledge: 'I had to concentrate on how to know my inner self and how to use it; on how other people lived or thought; and how the intricacies of nature wove into a harmonious whole.'[1]

While I was staying with the brothers of the Order of the Holy Cross in South Africa, a young man was going through the traditional initiation rites that mark the transition to manhood in his culture. He was in his hut on the edge of the property, and although of course I did not see him – all women are rigidly excluded during this time – I knew what was happening. Customs and traditions are firmly established in Xhosa tribal life, so that as a person moves from childhood to teenage years to adulthood to middle age and finally to old age, each step has its dress, its songs and dances. They believe that this age grouping brings stability to the social structure and establishes a succession of responsibilities and obligations. The young *umkhetha* was experiencing the initiation rite into manhood that was essentially based on circumcision, and involved exclusion from all tribal life until the cut healed. Then the young men would emerge with new clothes (particularly noticeable were the tweed caps) and with white clay on their faces, in public demonstration of their new status in society. Although this may seem far from any Western experience, it gave me a powerful image. With the young men wrapped only in blankets, and in the simplicity of huts specially built of branches that would later be burned, this time of initiation required poverty and nakedness, or near nakedness. There is a sense of being re-born, divesting oneself, becoming a *tabula rasa* ready to be filled with the knowledge and wisdom of the tribe. It seemed to me that there was a parallel here with the novice, who on admission to the community lies prostrate on the ground, saying *Suscipe me*, accept me, receive me, here I am empty before God in order to receive.

There is this same almost physical quality in the blessing that the mother in the Hebrides would give to the son or daughter who was leaving home:

Be the great God between thy two shoulders
To protect thee in thy going and in thy coming.

A ritual for letting a son or daughter go free, handing them over, under the protection of God, is not something that we naturally include as a part of growing up today in the West; yet we are here reminded of one of the most important steps of all of the transitions in life, moving from the confines of the family into freedom and maturity.

Death

As the time of death draws closer, there is this same sense of confidence in the abiding presence of a God who is alongside us and has walked every step of the way with us. Therefore, there is nothing remote or abstract in the blessings that, in their own words, are asked before 'crossing the black river of death; the great oceans of darkness; and the mountains of eternity'. For while a funeral is an event shared by family and friends, the time of dying is uniquely personal. Keeping watch beside the bedside of an old woman as she was dying, I found that these deathbed blessings, as I recited them time and again, had a sense of being outside of time, and their constant repetition enhanced their timeless quality. Many, as this one, have a strong sense of passage, and although ultimately that passing over from this life is made alone, those who have preceded us, the saints and the angels, are waiting to bring us to God.

Be each saint in heaven,
Each sainted woman in heaven,
Each angel in heaven
Stretching their arms for you,
Smoothing the way for you,
When you go thither
Over the river hard to see;
Oh when you go thither home
Over the river hard to see.[2]

If we begin to see the world in this way, then nightfall and sleep become reminders of that final crossing over, which will in the end bring us from sleep and death into light and life.

Be this soul on Thine arm, O Christ,
Thou King of the City of Heaven.[3]

Embracing change

If we are going to see life as a succession of thresholds to be crossed, we are reminded of the journeys of the people of Israel in the desert, and we then find symbols and images that we can apply to our own experience. The very words *passover* and *exodus* carry a fullness of meaning as a journey from bondage into freedom. It is important to remember that the passover was a yearly ritual, so that its memory was kept alive and the cycle lived through time and time again:

> As we sing our own song of Freedom
> by practicing the Art of Passingover
> . . . gradually the face of our life begins to change;
> it becomes face of freedom.[4]

The psalms are the journey songs of the people who made that passage. Time and again they raised a fist to God and shouted angrily at him, asking him where his will was in their lives. Had he forgotten or betrayed his faithful people? If we try to sanitize, edit, or sentimentalize the psalms, they lose their power. They are the songs of a people who were moving away from a known situation into the unknown, and they were often angry with a God who removed all those certainties, who instead seemed to be leading them along an apparently precarious path. They did not sit down for long beside gently flowing streams or linger in lush meadows. When we pray the psalms as they did, we, too, are compelled to stay 'at the raw edge', in the words of Walter Brueggemann.[5]

In the Gospels we watch a Christ who, in dismissing certainties, shows us what freedom might mean. We watch the way in which he enters into people's lives and *dissolves* an existing situation, whatever it might be. The likelihood was that the condition had promised security, safety, but now Christ challenges the people to *leave* their nets, or to *leave* a nice safe booth, and follow him. He says to Peter, James, and John, 'Come,' and to Matthew, 'Stand up, move, walk, come with me.' Our God is a God who moves and he invites us to move with him. He wants to prise us away from anything that might hold us too securely: our careers, our family systems, our money making. We must be ready to disconnect. There comes a time when the things that were undoubtedly good and right in the past must be left behind, for there is always the danger that they might hinder us from moving forward and connecting with the one necessary thing, Christ himself.

When Brueggemann writes about the Jewish people at one historic point in their story, the sacking of Jerusalem and the loss of the temple in 597, he uses the word *relinquish*.[6] It becomes a metaphor for the opening up to the new gifts and new forms of life given by God that become possible just when everything seems to have come to an end. Of course there is loss and it is right to grieve and not to pretend otherwise. Insecurity makes certitude attractive, and it is in times like these that I want to harness God to my preferred scheme of things, for it is risky to be so vulnerable. Yet it is this vulnerability that asks for trust and hope in God's plans, not mine. So I try to learn each time that I am called upon to move forward to hand over the past freely, putting it behind me, and moving on with hands open and ready for the new.

In the garden Christ gently but deliberately says to Mary Magdalene, '*Noli me tangere*': 'Do not touch' is a misleading translation that deprives us of the significance of what is happening here. 'Do not cling' is a more accurate rendering of the Greek, for surely we *do* need to touch, to touch the hem of the garment, to touch the wounds and feel them. But we must not *cling*, for that carries the danger of becoming dependent, of clutching or holding on in the wrong way. I love the statue of the Walking Madonna by Elisabeth Frink in the cathedral close at Salisbury. Here is this young woman who strides out boldly into the future, her one hand strong and determined, while the other is vulnerable. She knows that she has seen the Lord, the risen Christ; she has heard the resurrection message and now she is ready to cross the threshold and engage whatever lies before her.

What gives her the strength to move forward with today: such assurance, calling out that loving welcome, that *Deo Gratias*, to a future that is unsure, unknown?

Interlude: Crossing over with Saints and Angels

The barriers go down between this world and the next. Celtic blessings and rituals carry the African sense of 'the living dead', an idea wonderfully expressed in this twentieth-century Welsh poem, suggesting St David's presence on the soil of Wales today:

> There is no barrier between two worlds in the Church,
> The Church militant on earth
> Is one with the Church triumphant in heaven,
> And the saints are in this Church which is two in one.[1]

The saints accompany us on our journeys. The angels move easily between heaven and earth. There is constant crossing between two worlds. 'A hill touches an angel', in the words of Dylan Thomas, a Welsh poet *par excellence*, and there are more attributions to St Michael with all his angels in this area than in the rest of the country. Bucolic angels smile from tombstones in the churchyard or look down on us from funerary tablets on church walls as we sit in the pew below them. In the priory church at Abergavenny, the giant wooden figure of Jesse lies on his side while the angel at his head keeps watch:

The angel at his head is awake to see for him . . .
Jesse need not wake yet
With amazement, the angel
sees.[2]

The Revd Francis Kilvert, the nineteenth-century country
parson and diarist who lived here in the Welsh borders,
came to know his people and their local traditions well.
In one of his parishes, he was told that the people used to
gather on Easter morning 'to see the sun dance and play
in the water and the angels who were at the Resurrection
playing backwards and forwards before the sun'. They
were not serving any useful purpose, as the local poet
Ruth Bidgood tells us in her poem 'Resurrection Angels',
they were not there for healing, they were at play – and in
their dancing and playing they touched something in each
of the onlookers:

To and fro went the wings, to and fro
over the water, playing before the sun.
. . .
The people had no words to tell
the astonishment, the individual bounty –
for each his own dance in the veins,
brush of wings on the soul.[3]

4

Connecting Inner and Outer

The inner cloister

In his book *Living on the Border of the Holy*, a title that is itself significant, William Countryman writes of that border country that we all carry within us. He describes it as a kind of fault line that runs right down the middle of our lives. We can of course ignore it but it does not go away. We all live with it and we all have our unique experience of it, for it is part of who we are as human beings. It connects the surface or the ordinary reality with its deeper roots; indeed, he would actually claim that the border country is the realm in which human existence finds its meaning:

> This border country is a place of intense vitality. It does not so much draw us away from the everyday world as it plunges us deeper into a reality of which the everyday world is like the surface . . . To live there for a while is

like having veils pulled away. In the long run we find
that the border country is in fact the place we have
always lived, but it is seen in a new and clearer light.
Stay at the border, in active conversation with the holy
and the everyday.[1]

If we now return to St Benedict's portrait of the porter
waiting at the gates, we could almost say that this shows
us a conversation between the holy and the everyday
– between the inner enclosure with its life of prayer and
the exterior world with all its distractions and demands.
How do we hold the two together? How do we have a
conversation and not a confrontation? The porter shows
us what makes possible this strong, warm act of welcome. We see this figure of *stability*, someone who does
not go wandering off, either literally or metaphorically.
He is firmly rooted in this place, in himself. It is from this
firm internal centre that the external can be greeted and
welcomed, however strange, even challenging, it might
appear. The porter gives us the image of standing on the
threshold between two worlds.

The demands of the enclosure, with its times of prayer
and silence, ask for those qualities of commitment and
continuity, which bring a strong underpinning not only
to the Benedictine life but to any fulfilled and balanced
life. The cloister itself gives us such an amazing image
that I return to it time and again. What other complex of
buildings has the audacity to put emptiness at its heart?
It originates in the eighth century when the cloister and
the church were established as the two essential elements
of the monastic buildings. Since then it has taken many
forms and variants, as in Namibia where the Tutsing
Missionary Benedictine sisters have recently built a clois-

ter whose walkways open out at each of the four corners so that the community should never feel separated from the mountainside on which the monastery is built. In contrast, when John Pawson came to design a new monastery for a Cistercian community, Novy Dvur, in the Czech Republic, he gave them a glassed-in cloister in order to withstand the bitterly cold winters. Since the barrel vault is cantilevered there is no need for columns. At the base of the elongated windows runs a sculptured cast-concrete channel that collects rainwater, with a trough that throws glints of reflected sunlight into the vaulted ceiling. Here is the timeless, traditional cloister passageway presented in a starkly contemporary form.

To walk slowly around the four sides of a cloister, whether they were built today or in the Middle Ages, can tell us much about how emptiness and stillness at the heart of life can be achieved.

These passageways play a practical purpose that is also symbolic. They link all those buildings that serve the daily needs of a life that recognizes the demands of body, mind, and spirit – the holding together of the physical self with its need for sleep and food (the dormitory and the refectory); the self of the mind (the library where the intellect comes into play, and the chapter house where matters of day-to-day administration, finance, and business are handled, requiring the use of the intelligence); and finally the spiritual self (the church or the oratory). In the end, one might say that this whole balance of the three elements is actually dependent on the church, for it is the time and place for prayer that is the one essential priority that anchors everything else. Sleeping, eating, studying, manual work, decision making – all these other activities flow in and out of the work of God, the *opus Dei*. Prayer is the unifying foundation that maintains everything else in equilibrium. Muddle, confusion, being pulled first in one direction and then another, militate against a life with any sense of rhythm or unity. But here we see how living – however busy daily work may be – and praying can now become one continuous flowing movement, so that life is whole, a unified whole, in which no one thing is set above or apart from another.

Around that central open space run the arches, the succession of columns or pillars that carries the inner sides of the cloister walkways. Constantly changing according to the times of the day, the seasons of the year, they present us with a variety of amazingly varied and beautiful shadow patterns. Would there be the same perspective without these shadows? That is a good question to ask. It brings me back to the earlier theme of the light and the dark and the interplay of the two.

A gardener who travelled widely to write a book on monastic gardens was struck by the cloister garth, or garden, of this central space, open to the heavens, tunnelling daylight into the heart of the monastery. He noticed how often members of a community liked to sit in the cloister at twilight, reading by the last rays of daylight before Compline. He reflected on the importance of the presence of light, together with the presence of the green of grass and flowers, and above all the fountain or spring that brings a quiet and continuous undercurrent of sound to the whole:

Living in a building with good light is mentally uplifting ... The setting of green grass within the cloister range has long been known to have a unique power and grace and to exert a kind of subliminal attraction

. . . cloister garths create green oases of safety, simplicity, and purity.[2]

As I apply these comments to my own inner self, I am
reminded of the importance of keeping a garden watered
and fresh throughout all the differing times of the day
and the changing seasons of the year. For it is the water
in the centre that furnishes the most significant image; it
is the refreshment of the spring of living water that keeps
the garden green and gives it life.

Passing over and coming back

There are so many ways of describing this still centre:
the cave of the heart, the hidden poustinia, the innermost
cloister. Each one of us has our own picture. Essentially
it is that deep place where God finds us and we find him.
It is not empty space per se; its purpose is to become the
space for listening to the Word. We enter into silence and
hear God's conversation and take our proper part in it
– and if we heed ancient wisdom, that means trying not
to say too much ourselves.

But it is the centre from which we move outwards.
Monastic men and women, Thomas Merton above all,
describe themselves as people who are marginal, who
are living on the edges, and yet they are also the most
profoundly centred. As I think about the centre and the
edges in my own life, I ask myself about the relationship
of the two. Are the edges not perhaps the centre? Does the
centre not hold the edges? Perhaps it is just simply finding
the right connection of the two, the right way of coming
and going.

If the borders are not frontiers, and if the thresholds are continually crossed and re-crossed, then we open up to the new. John Dunne reminds us that: 'We all have this capacity to pass over and to come back again to ourselves, but we do not all discover it or learn how to use it.' He then goes on to say: 'I feel able to pass over into the other and come back again with new insights to my own.'[3]

Encountering new worlds

At the very end of his Rule when St Benedict encourages his followers, in an almost throwaway line about the need to continue reading and studying, he makes suggestions about what he would like them to study. It is one of the best examples of being told about preparing to open up to the new. For the two main sources that he proposes are taken from almost diametrically opposing perspectives, very different in their approaches. To explore divergent forms of monastic experience was not going to be a comfortable exercise. Yet the man who is looking for the welcome of the open door and the open heart is also looking for the open mind. The porter welcomes the stranger, who may be a visiting monk; the brothers who take him in are also ready to listen to him. It may well be that this man comes from some different tradition, but they accept that they can learn from what he says. To listen to everyone, whoever they may be, brother, child, fellow professional, is important. I like to think of this exchange as conversation; it is gentler than the word dialogue, which often carries a sense of confrontation. *A Vow of Conversation* is the title that Thomas Merton gave to his journals for the years 1964–65 and in his case it also becomes a play on words.[4] He is referring to *conversatio morum*, the vow of conversion of manners, to continual conversion and ongoing transformation in the life of a Trappist monk. But it also describes the way in which this solitary hermit loved to receive that stream of visitors who came from all walks of life and every sort of religious, philosophical, literary background to talk with him and exchange ideas. His vow of stability brought him rootedness both in the Trappist community at Gethsemani and also more profoundly in his own inner self. It gave him the place from which his interior journey could begin – breaking open new worlds, asking new questions, and unveiling new vistas. In the last year of his life he wrote of the need for 'effort, deepening, change, and transformation. Not that I must undertake a special project of self-transformation or that I must "work on myself" . . . let change come quietly and invisibly on the inside.'[5]

5

The Time Between Times

When he spent time in Thomas Merton's hermitage, the journalist and racial rights activist John Howard Griffin learned much about himself and his situation from being alone, living in great simplicity, dependent on the coming and going of light and dark:

> As you become more deeply attuned to the mystery of reality . . . it teaches you things you can hardly put into words, that can only be hinted by words, to abandon the self satisfaction of comfortable categories, to accept the unity of opposites (or contradictoriness) as the natural thing it is in reality.[1]

He found, as he knew that Merton did, that it was the times between times, and above all the hours before dawn, that were the most significant part of this mystery of reality. Here is the first entry in his diary as he established himself in the place where he was hoping to complete his biography of his old friend:

6 August 1969. 5.45 a.m. Before dawn.
 With the beginnings of predawn-light some of the birds come to life – not with singing yet, but with a kind of murmuring. I carried my coffee out on the concrete porch and drank it walking back and forth. The air is cool, almost cold, and fresh. Light came slowly. I watched the trees assume black shapes through the fog. I thought of Tom who saw the sounds, smelled the same predawn freshness, allowed the same silences to do their work in him.[2]

'The darkness before dawn' is one of Howard Griffin's favourite phrases as he himself begins the start of his day by waiting for the dawn, and finding what these hours can bring – 'hours of the rarest happiness when the silence, the dripping of the rain, the popping of the fire, and the blackness of night become prayer, and you are just there involved in all of that, your whole being saying the wordless amens . . .'[3] This was a time of 'emptying out', of cleansing, of getting rid of all the junk in body, mind, and senses, and it brought him the truest and deepest sense of wholeness and inter-connectedness.
 This is the predawn time, but there is also the time at dusk as well, when the light fades, the 'change-over routine' when evening falls, as I recalled earlier. This is particularly so in the winter:

 the sun has disappeared. Dusk is near – utter stillness outside, grey snows, greyer skies . . . I watch the cold landscape turning towards night . . . Long, long twilight. The light has scarcely dimmed outside, though some colour came into the sky through the woods to the west, a brilliant vermilion glow, startling in the greys ... The moments of early dawn and late dusk are similar in the qualities of silence they evoke, and everything in me defers to them.[4]

For twilight, the time between times, brings true grey, the colour that exists in its own right. Even the word itself, *twilight*, carries a gentle and lyrical sound, the time between lights, the greater light of the sun and the lesser light of the moon. Here is the moment of the changing of the guard between these two great luminaries. It is a fragile time of transition, half-light and half-dark – it is mysterious, ambiguous. It is the time of uncertainty, given to us daily as a reminder of the reality of the between-time.

It is an image from which we can learn so much, and it falls to the poet to tell us what this gift can mean. When Andrew Motion, the former Poet Laureate, was asked to turn *The Wind in the Willows* into a ballet libretto, he discovered an aura of mystery there that finds its way into these lines, spoken by the actor playing the author Kenneth Grahame as he emerges into the attic and looks around him at the audience:

> Here I am, just here. Awake
> But dreaming. In the attic of my home –
> And nothing is quite certain any more.
> Is this grey twilight or the dusty air?
> You see? You can't be sure. And nothing's sure.
> Inside my head. I'm like a ghost that floats
> Between two worlds . . .[5]

Recently when a nun in her mid-nineties sent me a note on my birthday, she quoted a line of Hegel: 'The owl of wisdom flies in twilight' and then said, 'I like to think that as we get older we live in two twilights; the evening twilight of letting-go and the dawn of looking forward. In both, Christ is our Light.' This makes me think of 'a kind of double vision in which we see both the light and the dark together and both sustain us', words actually taken from a book significantly entitled *Let Evening Come: Reflections on Aging*.[6]

Here is the giving up of the solace of certainty, for it means living with both/and. It is enjoying juxtaposition. It is embracing ambiguity. And if I recognize this poignant mix in my own inner landscape, ought I not let it shape my approach to the world around?

Each year we are given the chance to experience the power of the time between times, a reminder of the holiness of the pause, the space between. Yet it is generally neglected, misused. That most mysterious of all days, Holy Saturday, Easter Even, the day of Christ's descent into Hades, is most usually one of decorating the church, preparing Easter lunch, getting ready for a vacation. A priest who drew back from all this parochial busyness and communal jollity wrote:

Lord, they will scold me.

Today I did not appear
at the men's breakfast,
the children's egg hunt.
I dared not disturb
this great silence
with bacon or chocolates,
the savory, sweet minutiae
of parish life.

Today I need,
in simple solitude,
to live Your absence,
let it sweeten Your return,
make real Your presence
at tomorrow's festal feast.

This is the time of vital silence that gives meaning to the whole. It is like the silences in an orchestral performance that create the spaces between musical phrases and make the harmony possible. In her poem *Holy Saturday*, Bonnie Thurston reflects on this day on which 'Nobody can be sure what will happen next.'

I love this day
of silent waiting
when fasting is over,
but feasting not begun,
when pain is past
but flesh not quickened.
This is where we live,
this human place,
waiting before the cave
in the tarnished garden
where it all began
and ended
to begin anew,
we hope, forever.

This is where we live, she claims. But is it? To wait, to keep vigil, to be ready with attentive listening? She writes of the role of uncertainty:

Nobody can be sure
what will happen next.[7]

The costliness of being open

To be comfortable with uncertainty today requires courage. Elsewhere I have written about asking questions rather than finding answers, about being content with hints and guesses, about the importance of mystery. When I reflect on the changes that I have witnessed in recent years in South Africa, I see a country in which earlier certainties have dissolved, for in the years of apartheid people were clearly ranged on either side of issues; they knew where they stood, they had banners and slogans and allies. Each side was convinced of the morality of the stand they were taking. Those in the expensive white suburbs of Johannesburg did not venture into the black township of Soweto.

'We must try and make space for ambiguity.' These words were said in the recent post-apartheid era by none other than Wilhelm Verwoerd, the grandson of the architect of apartheid – the 'architect of Separate Development', Dr Hendrick Verwoerd. Antjie Krog, in her powerful account of the Truth and Reconciliation Commission, which under Archbishop Desmond Tutu heard the testimonies of the victims of abuse and violence, tells how she once bumped into Wilhelm Verwoerd, the young philosophy professor. He smiled at her and said, 'I had wanted to give you a quote: If truth is the main casualty in war, ambiguity is another . . . One of the legacies of war is a habit of simple distinction, simplification and opposition . . . which continues to do much of our thinking for us.' When her companion asked him what he meant by this he elaborated: 'It means that in the past we had no choice but to live by simple white or black guidelines. But we shouldn't continue being dictated to by oversimplified credos during times of peace. We must try and make space for ambiguity.'[8] Significantly, the final chapter of his autobiographical account of the change of heart that led to his joining the ANC (the African National Congress, the spearhead of the struggle against apartheid) is entitled 'A Commitment to Continuing Conversion'.[9]

'We are not sinning if we are unsure of the answers to hard questions. We are sinning if we do not think or care.' These are the words of that most wise and holy man Michael Ramsey. Perhaps this was unthreatening to him because this was how he lived, because he was himself familiar with this mysterious boundary between life now and life eternal, between experience and hope, between sorrow and joy. In 1966, when he was Archbishop of Canterbury, he wrote a small book called *Problems of Christian Belief* in which he spoke of the pattern of 'alternating night and day' in his own life:

> Christian faith has been for me a constant process of wrestling, of losing and finding, of alternating night and day. For me the struggle is not between faith and unbelief so much as within faith itself. Faith is a sort of adventurous conflict in the midst of which certainty deepens. When the certainty passes, as it does for me, into a sense of peace and serenity it is none the less a costly peace, a peace in the heart of conflict.[10]

Struggling with the challenge of the bitter tension and deep-rooted hatred that was breaking up society in

Northern Ireland, a Methodist minister recently wrote of the inspiration and immediate implications he found as he reflected on the Trinity, not as a philosophical and speculative problem but as a practical experience to be lived:

> In this vision of God there is real diversity in unity and unity in diversity. The three-one God is a community of mutuality, equality and reciprocity. . . . This vision of God critiques and challenges all our separatist, isolationist, sectarian division, and its exclusion and excluding zones. It calls us beyond the idea of benign apartheid or coexistence. Diversity in unity and unity in diversity, mutuality, equality, interdependence and interrelationships, are ultimate realities because they are of the very essence of God, who is Trinity.[11]

This is an encounter of hospitality in all its fullness. It is found in all traditional societies, and it is given very simple and profound expression in the portrait that St Benedict draws in his Rule of the porter – on whom we are also to model ourselves. His welcome carries blessing: *Benedicite! Thanks be to God that you are here.* But true hospitality is one of both giving and receiving. As the well-known Benedictine writer Sr Joan Chittister paraphrases it, 'Thank God that someone has come to stretch our minds and souls. Thank God that someone has come to shake us out of our complacency. Thank God that someone has come to prod us beyond ourselves.'[12]

Whatever name we may choose – the time between, the threshold, the pause – it is by naming it that we honour it and thereby honour change, movement, difference. In his book, with the significant title *The Dignity of Difference*, the Chief Rabbi, Jonathan Sacks, writes:

Truth on earth is not, nor can it aspire to be, the whole truth . . . God is greater than religion . . . Can I recognise God's image in someone who is not in my image, whose language, faith, ideals are different from mine? If I cannot, then I have made God in my image instead of allowing him to remake me in his.[13]

He is telling us that God loves differences, as John Habgood, the former Archbishop of York, wrote when he was reviewing this book: 'Human and religious diversity is just as much in need of preservation as biological diversity.' After all, God called a particular people in order to teach all people the dignity of difference. 'Babel was a terrible mistake, not because God was in any way threatened by human achievement, but because humanity, with its new-found technological expertise, was attempting "to impose a man-made unity on divinely created diversity".'[14]

Listening means learning, and with that comes the willingness to change. When the Jesuit William Johnston lived in Japan, he began to listen to the voice of Buddhism, but because he was listening to two choruses he found he was beginning to ask questions. This was painful, for it opened up areas of consciousness that had previously lain dormant.[15]

The first step in listening, learning, and changing is to see that *different* is not dangerous; the second is to be happy and willing to live with uncertainty; the third is to rejoice in ambiguity and to embrace it. It all means giving up the comfort of certainty and realizing that uncertainty can actually be good. As soon as I realize this, I find that I must ask myself: what is my first task in approaching another people?

I have here set out my response as a meditation that

is simultaneously also a form of prayer. It is inspired by something I saw pinned up in a Roman Catholic convent in Harare, which makes it all the more poignant in the context of life in Zimbabwe today:

> My first task in approaching another people
> another culture
> another religion
> Is to take off my shoes.
> For the place that I am approaching is holy.
> Otherwise I may find myself
> treading on another's dreams,
> their memories, their stories,
> More serious still – I might forget
> that God was there . . .

I need to pause, to take time, when I find myself on the threshold of another culture. I need to remind myself that as I meet them they will be bringing all their baggage of tradition and history, of suffering and triumph. So first I need to take time to look into my own self, to find in myself a willingness to be vulnerable, honest about my own story, its roots and its past, confronting the reality without attempting to escape into fantasy or nostalgia. For when I am attentive to where I am standing, I will also be attentive to where the other is standing, and only then will I be truly prepared to listen to them. There is nothing more important than this. It sounds so easy. Yet it is demanding, and essential, for it is fundamental, foundational. It means listening, the totality of listening, not only with the ears but also with the eyes.

This is something that we find portrayed so amazingly in the icon of the Rublev Trinity – and perhaps only the non-verbal could take us into the depths that we need. Here we see the visit of the three angels to Abraham, receiving his hospitality under the oak of Mamre – but also the three members of the Trinity sitting round the table with the cup in the centre. The reverse perspective invites us all to enter and to partake of this company. We are not only observers, but also guests. We are drawn into this circle, we see those heads inclined toward one another, as they listen intently to each other, the hair drawn back so that the ear is exposed, as they look at one another 'with listening eyes', as someone once commented. Each holds the other in a gaze of the most profound acceptance and love. This is the gaze of openness with nothing judgmental here, no rivalry, nothing obsessional – rather a look of gratitude and shared delight.

How far?

I have been writing this book at my cottage in the Welsh Borders during the summer months, hoping to finish it by Lammas. I have gone constantly from my study to the orchard, the copse, the riverbank, taking with me my half-resolved thinking, and letting the rhythm between house and garden, inside and outside, work on me. Gardening in itself has about it something of this art of conversation. For my garden only exists through the 'conversation' between myself and the given quality of the land itself in its natural state. I try to respect and enhance this without dominating. I try to do enough clearing, letting in enough light, and removing the destructive forces, to allow a continual exchange between myself and the natural elements. I hope that from this something will emerge that

reflects a partnership between us. And since it is changing all the time, not only throughout the seasons but also
year by year, as old trees die or floods alter the shape of
the riverbanks, it will continue as an ongoing conversation in which both of us are involved. It is a reminder of
border life.

There is something unpredictable in life beside a stream
– which continuously changes its shape and configuration
– and it reminds me as I come to the end of this exploration of the image of the border that I must accept that
it cannot conclude with any clearcut picture. But living
with uncertainty is not the same as living with insecurity.
It is important to differentiate the two. I know where I
belong and where I am rooted, and with that firm base,
that centre, I can reach out, open up. Yet this inner space
is not some closely guarded 'sacred enclave', segregated
and safely behind barriers, but a place open to growth
and new life. I take to myself what Father Christian, the
French Trappist monk in Algeria, wrote from his experience of living in a monastic community in a country
where other cultures posed questions with which he had
to engage. He was addressing the general chapter of the
Cistercians in 1993, when he said these words, which
really sum up where this book has been taking me: 'Our
Christian identity is always in the process of being born.
It is a paschal identity.'[16]

Certainty can appear immensely attractive, appealing
both to individuals and to nations, particularly, in times
of suffering and distress. Complexity, ambiguity, untidi-
ness – these are very different. I have come to find that
they carry more conviction. The closed mind, the *laager*
mentality, is the greatest obstacle to any real freedom
– the freedom of openness. As soon as we admit that

there are no right answers, that we must be ready to live with contradiction, we are forced instead to listen to one another, to admit our need to learn, to recognize our need to receive.[17]

> Let us live with uncertainty
> as with a friend.
> To feel certain
> means feeling secure.
> To feel safe is unreal,
> a delusion of self.
> Knowing we do not know is
> the only certainty letting the self be lost into Christ.

These words, written anonymously by a monastic, speak of the courage and strength that come from this way of living. It may be a brave, even a foolhardy or risky undertaking, but if we choose to live on the borders we find ourselves part of a company of fellow travellers who are ready to say:

> For us there are no certainties, no star
> blazing our journey . . .
> We try
> out our way lit with angels, wondering
> 'How far?'[18]

Perhaps there is something prophetic about living on the border. I want a Christianity that brings me comfort, but also *dis*-comfort. In the new science I find a vocabulary that, even if I do not fully understand it, helps me to articulate my own thoughts.[19] The old world of Newtonian certainty drew lines and was happy with whatever was systematic, rational, and could be subjected to reason. Now in a world of inter-relatedness, 'connections work across the separations'. 'Senders and receivers' are linked together in a way that means energy, fertility, new birth. This is inevitably more complex and more demanding, just when I would like things to become smoother and simpler. Listening to other voices asks me not only to be attentive to the place where I stand and to ask questions of myself, but also to be open and willing to recognize where the other might bring in a corrective, a deepening or strengthening. Perhaps this will be painful, opening up areas of consciousness that previously were dormant. But in a two-way exchange the other has as much to give as I have to receive. Ideally the border should be the place of encounter and contrast that can lead, not to syncretism, but to a moving forward in greater fullness. It is a place that Church and society have never needed more.

God, who is there at the centre, is also at the raw edges. Our living God moves and expects us to move with him. God will not let us settle easily or for too long. Our God is too big for either/or. Instead he asks us to say both/and. So we move into that threshold to meet the God who is both known and unknown. The last pause of all is at the threshold of God who is unending mystery.

Afterword

Re-reading the landscape

Time and again, in the ten years since I first wrote this book, I have looked back and found that the idea that I had then begun to explore continued to resound in my mind, and that I wanted to take it further. I had been writing in those years at the end of the last century when the dawn of a new millennium seemed to promise so much. But now we watch escalating conflict and controversy, and instead of harmony we see divergence and dissonance. The growth of extremism and fundamentalism – political and religious – leads to polarization, and the ability to listen to one another seems to have diminished.

I had been describing an open and porous borderland in the Welsh Marches where peoples, traditions, and cultures met and mingled, challenging and learning from one another. It was like the juxtaposition of two voices, preventing either from becoming too safe or self-contained. This landscape had given me – since I had made the connection between the exterior landscape and my own interior landscape – an image of living with difference and diversity, accepting uncertainty. This theme had much in common with what Mark Tully was to say in a lecture given in Hereford Cathedral, very soon after the fall of the twin towers in New York on September 11th 2001. Under the title 'From Certainty to Uncertainty, from Dogma to Dialogue', he drew on his own experience of belonging to two worlds: the East and the West, India and England. He spoke of the importance of listening and learning from the other. He made a plea for the 'maybe this, maybe that' mentality that comes so naturally in India where people are suspicious of the dogmatic which they believe leads us into traps. The following summer he returned to this theme when he spoke on the vital role of difference and diversity at Hay-on-Wye (at the yearly festival which for ten days turns this small Welsh border town into an international scene for literature and the arts): 'Those who are dogmatic and certain that they are right don't feel vulnerable and have no desire to have conversations.'[1]

Place matters: we learn from the land. Increasing numbers of people recognize this and are writing about it.[2] For the seventeenth-century country parson, Thomas Traherne, living at Credenhill, outside Hereford, it was his sense of connectedness to the earth that transformed the world for him from being little more than 'heaps of things and happenings' into something that 'seemed to me all so extraordinarily wonderful'. His writings show his gift of seeing into the essence of a thing, seeing beyond the merely exterior. For him, whatever he encountered, from the miniature – an ant, a grain of sand – to the vast – the stars, the sea, the entire landscape – became revelatory.

As I think about this ability to look and see and listen, I ask myself whether this is a natural gift, or one that can be acquired. What does it ask of any of us to turn the landscape into a revelation? How can the land become a mentor? For an answer, I have turned – as I increasingly do – to the poets and artists, and not least to those who are associated with this local area (and whose works have been included in this revised book).

For Ruth Bidgood, the land

> has its own vocabulary
> half-alien; not another language
> but an unfamiliar dialect.

She calls it 'a language half-recognised', which asks of us to take time to listen:

> I hear the stony flow of the stream
> As speech, though not about anything
> I know.[3]

When Charles MacCarthy wanted to return to painting the Borders landscape, he tells us that he set about it obliquely, by painting the distant Welsh hills reflected in a set of windows. But recognizing just how complex the relationship to landscape is, he knew that distance must be balanced by what is close at hand. So each day he took the same path, going with his dog, through the same seven fields, over the same gate, past a churchyard, a stream . . . Only in this way could he become aware of those subtle changes in all the immediate textures and shapes lying within a half mile; aware of a living pulse that forms a continuum and a sense of ongoing communion, as important as the sight of those far distant hills. He says that he is grateful for John Constable's dictum that 'The landscape painter must walk in the fields with a humble mind. No arrogant man was ever permitted to see nature in all her beauty.'[4]

This process must be slow and gentle. I think of it in terms of an unveiling, or decoding, peeling back layer upon layer. Constable said that it will escape those who approach it arrogantly. I remember the poet Frances Horowitz, my neighbour for some years while she was living at Rowlestone mill, wandering through the lanes and climbing the hills around here, and how she expressed the same sense of reticence:

> we have encroached –
> this is not yet our land.[5]

Ansel Adams, who must rank as one of the greatest of photographers of the twentieth century through his portrayal of the dramatic landscape of western America, called a photograph an instrument of love and revelation, and said that it was essential for any sensitive photographer to 'come before reality more tenderly'. He said that a good photograph was like a good poem. It would say something now that, years later, would become an image saying something totally other.[6]

This is something that Thomas Merton understood well. Best known for his writings as a Trappist monk, Merton in his later years came to love photography, and used his camera so creatively that it became in his hands an instrument of contemplation. He told a young poet as they walked together in the woods around his hermitage, in the grounds of the abbey of Gethsemani, that he was far too quick, too greedy, and as a result took far too many photographs. He needed to become more open and receptive:

> 'You can't appreciate anything around you if you're always self-conscious, thinking, blotting out everything else but you.' As a result, an impatient young man, eager to seize and to possess, came away with far fewer pictures because he discovered that he must become attentive, waiting for the image to reveal itself.[7]

Approaching the land in order to receive and to learn, was more familiar in the past than today. Then, men and women living close to the earth cultivated their relationship with it, recognizing the demands that it made. There was nothing sentimental about it. Yet the words chosen by H. J. Massingham to describe his visit to an old man farming not far away from where I live, spoke of him as 'a man who paid his earth-dues religiously'. He called him 'a student of his native soil' and said that his 'practice was one of loving no less than learning. They came together in wisdom which is neither love nor learning but both in one.'[8] The experience of the professional landscape gardener probably comes closest to this today: 'Understanding a landscape is like getting to know a person. It is slow, you need time to draw out the personality.'[9]

✠

Re-reading my original book, in the context of what the artists and the poets have shown me, I realize that I had been approaching the landscape, as it were, from a horizontal perspective. Now I wanted to read it vertically. An ancient landscape is enigmatic and multi-layered, carrying centuries of myth and history, legend and story-telling. Here is another conversation, which asks me to listen to a succession of voices from many past times, simultaneously present and valid. This idea of the telescoping of time is expressed, in a totally different context, by Penelope Lively in a novel in which her central character, the 67-year-old Claudia, returns to a place that she has known when young. She finds it changed: there are now concrete and tower-blocks and tourists. Yet it is still the same. She stands on a pavement crying, not in grief but in wonder that nothing is ever lost, that everything can be retrieved, that a lifetime is not linear but instant. That, inside the head, everything happens at once.[10]

This border country is a 'peopled landscape', where the present does not obliterate the past. Merlin still sleeps

Church Gate and Yews by Edgar Holloway.

in Mynydd Merddin, Merlin's Mountain, while a few miles away stands Arthur's Stone, his royal seat, with its spectacular rocks overlooking a vast panorama stretching westwards. The name Gospel Pass, lying between Hay-on-Wye and the Black Mountains, recalls the story of St Peter and St Paul, arriving from Rome to evangelize this part of Britain. After casting lots, St Peter set out along the Golden Valley, where he has left his name in the village of Peterchurch, while St Paul came down over the high mountain pass into the Llanthony valley, thus reaching Capel-y-ffin. This tiny hamlet, whose name means 'place on the boundary', was later to attract two unusual communities.

First, it became home to Fr Ignatius, the eccentric Victorian monk, who wanted to restore the religious life to the Anglican Church, and was idealistic enough to build a monastery here. He is still commemorated in a pilgrimage in his honour which, once a year, brings his devotees to his gaunt, ruinous church. But the monastery survived, and it was its remote and beautiful location that drew Eric Gill, his family, and David Jones here in the 1930s. For both these men it became a place in which their creativity flourished, and for David Jones, in particular, memories of the features of these local hills continued to influence his later works. The years they spent here served them both well for they came looking for something and they found it. They are supreme examples of the idealization of the Borders, of seeing what they wanted to find. They turned their back on the suffering of the industrialized valleys, lying only a few miles away. They did not think that the quiet of a romantically empty valley might have been purchased by poverty and de-population. They associated the wild ponies roaming the hillsides with the

Wild Ponies by David Jones.

legend that they were the descendants of King Arthur's cavalry which ran free after his defeat; they did not associate them with the pit ponies of the mines at Blaenavon.

For below its peaceful surface this borderland carries scars. It has seen every sort of loss and grief and suffering, whether in social and economic life, or in the bloodshed of battle and conflict. The writer Ronald Blythe once said, in a sermon given at Cambridge, that 'one of the things which is very disturbing in our own day in which such appalling violence has occurred – unprecedented violence towards humanity, such cruelties, such barbarities – is that nothing cries out in the landscape.' But then he added significantly: 'I think that is because we have not really learnt to read it properly.'[11] Perhaps things are better forgotten. Who, standing in the calm of the quire of Dore Abbey, would guess that when the high altar was

consecrated in 1282 by that godly man St Thomas Canti-
lupe, it had to take place in the presence of armed guards
because of the wrangles between the diocese of Hereford
and the diocese of St Davids?

The sites of two other churches, which date back to the
earliest years of Christianity here, also appear tranquil
enough. Yet both are places commemorating death. Here
we remember two local saints who died for their faith:
one a hermit slain by brigands, the other a royal prince
killed in battle. Partrishow, where the hermit St Issui lived
a solitary life, continues to draw pilgrims today as it has
done for centuries, and the holy well hidden in the slope
below the church carries prayer flags and small crosses
left by those who have visited it to pray and to seek healing. And there is Clodock, which in English sounds rustic
enough. Its Welsh name, Merthyr Clydawg, however,
reminds us that this is the burial site of another martyr,
a prince called Clydawg, who was killed in battle. Here
was a prince who 'led in battle and prayer', in the words
of Ruth Bidgood. Here, then, is another 'place of shifting boundaries,/ strife, loss, perpetual haunting, garbled
names . . .'.[12] The border is particularly explicit here for
above the church the horizon is marked by the long line
of Offa's Dyke, which runs along the escarpment of the
Black Mountains. It was the work of the eighth-century
Mercian King Offa, proud contemporary of the Emperor
Charlemagne, who in building this giant earthwork to
mark the limits of his kingdom against the barbarians to
the west has also immortalized his own name.

The gift of a 'peopled landscape' is that it does not
allow those of us who live here today to forget those
others who lived here in the past. It is above all as we
place our feet on the earth that we really become aware

of this. Somewhere Ronald Blythe has said that anyone who *walks* never walks through a landscape alone, 'for the people of the past are present, right beside him'. The land carries their names, whether they are historical or mythical, English or Welsh: a portrait gallery of men and women whose lives were inextricably part of the life lived here. Many, such as St Issui or St Clydawg – and there are many more – were Celtic saints and hermits, who gained their sainthood not because of any official ecclesiastical process but through local acclamation: the recognition of the neighbourhood that the places associated with them had been changed by their dedicated lives of prayer. For them, living in their solitary cells and isolated hermitages, there was only one boundary running through their lives: their commitment to living in the borderland between this

The Skirrid by Charles MacCarthy.

world and the next. Their lives held together the boundary between heaven and earth. When the twentieth-century Welsh poet Gwenallt writes about St David, Dewi, still present and moving among his people, he says:

> There is no barrier between two worlds in the Church,
> The Church militant here on earth
> Is one with the Church triumphant in heaven,
> And the saints are in this Church which is two in one,
> They come to worship with us, our small
>   congregation,
> The saints our oldest ancestors
> Who built Wales on the foundation
> Of the Crib, the Cross and the Empty tomb.[13]

But finally, more ancient still, the hills themselves carry their stories. From my kitchen window I look out towards Graig Syfyrddin, the Hill of the Seraphim, a reminder of the presence of crowds of angels moving easily between heaven and earth. Its gently rising slope stands in stark contrast to the sharp outline of the Skirrid, which is known locally as the Holy Mountain. The reason is, it is said, that its dramatically scarred side occurred at the third hour of the crucifixion, when rocks crashed down in a great landslide as the whole world mourned the death of Christ. Here is time outside time, time which challenges attachment to chronological time.

For surely Merlin and Offa and St Issui and Thomas Traherne, the timeless angelic hosts, and events of Good Friday, are all here and all with a valid part to play in that inter-connectedness which builds up the whole. David Jones clearly felt this, and it can be seen very vividly in his painting of the crucifixion set in the Llanthony valley. The cross itself is made from branches hewn from nearby trees whose raw stumps are clearly visible in the foreground. A pigeon-like bird flies past, and one of the local wild ponies is cropping the grass. Above is written the legend: Sanctus Christus de Capel-y-ffin.[14]

Here David Jones is siting the first century within the twentieth. The figure of the Green Man, however, which is omnipresent in this area, takes us back to the pre-Christian era. Here is a human face, peering through the foliage which sprouts from the mouth, with eyebrows growing into branches and tendrils which cover the head. This is an image that speaks of the livingness of matter, the essential goodness of creation, and the inter-relationship of the human with the natural. Handed down from one generation to another by local artisans and carvers, craftsmen in wood and stone, it was an entirely visual tradition. It gives us a glimpse of a whole world of inner, secret knowledge, a crossing of the divides of time and place, carried on without any written word. The Green Man may appear in the wooden screen of some tiny chapel; become the capital of a twelfth-century stone arch, supporting a tympanum of Christ in Majesty, as at Rowlestone; or be translated into a magnificent boss high in the vault of a Cistercian abbey in the later middle ages, as at Dore. Clearly the twelfth-century builders of a small local church found no difficulty in associating him with the figure of Christ, just as later medieval monks found no difficulty in having him above their heads as they sang their daily offices. But this should hardly surprise us, for is not the natural creation one of those links which crosses over and breaks down the barriers of time, place, and belief?

✠

There is nothing clear cut and simple in this border country. The land itself, which ought, quite literally, to be the most down-to-earth of any topic to write about, is yet proving otherwise. It speaks in a voice that is complex, elusive. It takes time to listen to it, layer upon layer, in contrast to walking the streets of London, or any other city or town, where the pavements make statements which can be read easily. The inscription on a drain cover will tell me exactly by whom it was made and where. It is spelt out: 'Ham Baker & Co. Ltd, Fire Hydrant, Westminster', or 'Winser & Co, Inspection Cover, Buckingham Palace Rd, London'. It alerts me to the fact of a network of public utilities lying below my feet. But here in the Borders, the ground under my feet is the source not of certainty, but rather of mystery.

It is with this sense of mystery in mind that I will set out, alone or with a small group of friends, to walk along the Cwm brook, which runs below my garden. We stop at intervals to read poetry written by poets who have lived in the Borders and been inspired by them, and who can heighten our capacity to see and to feel what may lie hidden beneath our feet or all around us. We walk slowly, consciously aware of our surroundings, ready to stop, to gaze, not merely glancing quickly or superficially. A phrase of Ruth Bidgood's expresses what otherwise might elude us: 'correspondences, patterns, astonishments'. Her word *astonishment* is the key: it opens us up to wonder and amazement, it brings delight, it leads into gratitude.

In an address to the David Jones Society Conference in London, in 2008, Rowan Williams said:

To be *here* and not *there*, in this landscape, this country, literally – Britain, Wales – is to be inevitably connected with the many times that there are in this one place; and to be intelligent, to be a cultural being, in this one place is to be listening for those times and those differences that are there in the one place.

The idea of being at home, in one place, while yet part of a wider horizon is one of the themes of this book. The particular opens out into the universal. To realize great matters in a small space is something familiar in Welsh. Waldo Williams, the early twentieth-century poet, gives a classical statement:

Cael neuadd fawr
Rhwng cyfyng furiau

When Rowan Williams translates these lines – 'Inhabiting a great hall/ between narrow walls' – he says that they give us a definition of life itself.[15] Here we have the great in the small, the universal in the immediate. As another contemporary poet who lives in Wales, Anne Cluysenaar, says: 'The near and the far are held in tension; the immediate landscape takes on a new, metaphorical significance when it is embraced as part of a wider world . . .'[16]

Being *here* is therefore no restriction. The monastic understanding of stability never becomes static for it is linked to the commitment to continual change and transformation. So when I ask if this landscape is the same as ten years ago, or is it different, I know that I myself am different. I am always changing, a quiet opening up to the new that perhaps I do not fully recognize until I need to articulate it. This means that the way in which I now 'read' the landscape reflects what I have been thinking about and trying to explore in my writing and teaching.

One of the pleasures of this stage of one's life is the way

in which all the threads of the tapestry begin to converge. Now, as I look back, past and present begin to merge and bring a new wholeness, a unity. I want to pay homage to the past which laid the foundation. My father, an enthusiastic local antiquarian, gave me my first training as a historian, and taught me how to look at church buildings. When I became a history student at Cambridge, I learned the importance of being faithful to the text, and I was given the tools for sound, academic critical use of the sources. Then I escaped from the confines of verbal and written evidence, and went on to discover the role of the visual, the un-written. But how could I know, in those years, as a young woman walking parish boundaries and looking at field systems, dating brickwork, using aerial photography, that poetic awareness or the mythic and symbolic dimension of the landscape might one day come to have a role to play? As I have turned to poets and to artists for illumination, I have inevitably become increasingly aware of the importance of the imagination, of the role of image and symbol.[17]

The image above all that a border country presents is that of the threshold, the place of crossing over. In the years since this book was first published, that threshold image has come to hold a much greater significance since I have been thinking about baptism, which is essentially the crossing of a threshold, from an old self to a new self, a new way of life. I now realize why the Hereford Mappa Mundi, the medieval map in which the world is centred on Jerusalem, since its purpose is theological rather than geographical, gives such prominence to the Red Sea. It stands out like some terrible red gash, arresting one's attention, out of all proportion. For this is, after all, the great threshold moment in the experience of the people of Israel, which is paralleled in the Christian life at the river Jordan, 'the beginning of the new order of the Spirit'.[18] The Red Sea is the passage from the old to the new, as is also the Jordan: the boundary, the gateway into freedom.

The older I grow, the more important this becomes, and I find that I re-visit the succession of thresholds in my past life. I try to see if I was attentive to them. I ask myself if I crossed them mindfully or unmindfully? Was I aware that there was grace to be found there? Sr Renée Branigan OSB, who reviewed the American edition of this book[19] and with whom I was subsequently in correspondence, asked some interesting questions:

> Since most of growing up is a spiral progression, do we expect to return to the threshold; if so, is it the same or different?
>
> Is patience a threshold virtue?
>
> How porous are thresholds? Do they entertain a flow both ways?
>
> Can we cross thresholds in retrospect?

She says that she does not know the answers. Nor do I. But I do know that the succession of thresholds is an inescapable part of life for each one of us, and that each must be faced and lived out with courage and with sensitivity.

Here then is uncertainty, the not knowing what lies ahead. But it is not the same as insecurity, an important distinction. It is only because I am firmly earthed and grounded that I can stand so firmly, ready to move forward into the unknown, and open myself up to new questions, new explorations. This is the gift of stability, the virtue of being rooted and grounded, which in his excellent grasp of the human psyche St Benedict has

made the cornerstone of life as he set it out in the Rule
– wisdom which applies not merely to his followers but
to us all. Mark Tully demonstrated this well when, at the
Hay festival in 2002, he spoke about the importance of
achieving the balance that will enable us to welcome the
new while still being part of what is left behind. 'You do
need to stand firmly on your own two feet, for it is that
which will enable us to move forward and will allow the
opening up of yourself to the winds of the world.'

✠

The last weeks in which I have been finishing this book
have seen untimely rain, with mist and cloud, and only
glimpses of the sun. The outline of the Hill of the Seraphim is there as I stand at the kitchen window, and then
moments later it has disappeared. I am grateful for the
elusive quality of this landscape. It is part of its given-ness.
The American writer Luci Shaw was surprised to find that
this was the landscape that spoke to her rather than the
drama of the high mountains of North Wales: 'I thought
I loved the hard, bright edges best/ until I walked into
this morning's mist.' It is a vivid expression of presence
and absence, of living with vulnerability, without clarity
and certainty, while yet paradoxically being grounded in
strength and an inner security. Light and dark, and the
exchange between them, are written out for us endlessly
in this landscape, as the Revd Francis Kilvert, the Victorian diarist, recorded on a spring day in the Llanthony
valley, in 1870: 'The Black Mountains were invisible,
being wrapped in cloud . . . cloud and mist roll away . . .
The mountains stand up in clear blue heaven.'[20]
 I hope, therefore, that although this book might appear

to be about one specific place, the Welsh borderland, those who read it will be willing to address it at the level of image and symbol, and make the connection between the exterior and their own inner landscape. I know no better example of this than the monastic life of Thomas Merton, set in the rolling hills of Kentucky, a far cry from the hills and valleys of the Welsh Borders. But here we can see how the exterior and the interior can relate. For Merton was in his early years rootless and homeless, a wanderer, living in France, in England, in New York and belonging nowhere. But when he entered the Trappist monastery of Gethsemani, the stability of his monastic vocation gave him what he so desperately longed for, 'the love of one good place'. Only then, from this commitment that brought him the sense of being rooted and earthed, could he begin his true interior journey, his life's vocation. Someone who understands him well has written perceptively of this: 'He passed over to the true geography of his heart – not by crossing seas and seeking out new cities, but by sinking roots in one place . . . Rooting his mind at Gethsemani he paradoxically experienced the wider horizons of his time.'[21]

This small book offers an invitation to visit the borderland of your own interior landscape and spend time there. I conclude with what I always say to anyone who sets out to walk with me, and with the poets whom we will share, along the Cwm brook:

> To listen visually to the landscape here is a quiet dialogue, which asks for reverence and respect, taking time. But it brings the opportunity of exploration at many levels, not least a personal interior journey.
>
> Are you ready to join me on this exploration?

Passages for Reflection

Living on the border

The border state is a social and cultural phenomenon. But it is rich in metaphysical possibilities too. It may be seen as a boundary between worlds, a frontier between the living and the dead, the seen and the unseen, surface and depth, language and silence.

Jeremy Hooker, 'Putting the Poem in Place', Inaugural Professorial Lecture, University of Glamorgan (2007), 15

Man is a borderer. He is the sole inhabitant of a tract of country where matter marches with spirit.

David Jones, *Epoch and Artist* (London: Faber, 1959), 86

In the border country one discovers connections, roots, limits, *meaning*. To live there for a long while is like having veils pulled away.

L. William Countryman, *Living on the Border of the Holy: The Human Priesthood and the Church* (Harrisburg, PA: Morehouse Publishing, 1978)

Living with difference

Identities that are woven are always, if you take that metaphor seriously, constructed not out of nothing but out of the awareness of ourselves, each one of us, as a place where immeasurable differences intersect . . . It is to recognise that one's self is also a layered and broken reality.

Rowan Williams, Chapter IV: 'Shaping Holy Lives' in *The Oblate Life*, ed. Gervase Holdaway OSB (Norwich: Canterbury Press, 2008)

In our culture one criterion becomes dominant: the criterion of what is 'comfortable' for us. This plaintive word crops up everywhere. 'I am not comfortable with this. I am not comfortable with that . . .' Once comfort becomes the test for reality, we risk imprisonment within the self. Encounter with otherness, engagement with what is strange and different, can seldom be comfortable . . .

Martin L. Smith SSJE, *Nativities and Passions* (London: Darton, Longman & Todd, 1996; Cambridge, MA: Cowley Publications, 1995), 59

Living with space

There must be a continuing dialogue between men and women and space, because this is a part of what it means to be human.

Ambrose Wathen, 'Space and Time in the Rule', *Cistercian Studies*, 1992, XVII, 1

Where is the centre of the universe for you? We need a centre to make sense of the whole. The human person stands in need of a centre so as to experience his or her life as oriented.

John Eudes Bamberger, 'On Defining the Centre', *Cistercian Studies*, 1980, XV, 382

This is the timeless question as we all try to explore: the interplay between the temporal and the eternal. The question is, 'How does one live out of a transfigured centre?'

E. de W. adapting something said by Cynthia Bourgeault, based on the *Navigatio Santi Brendani Abatis* (The Voyage of St Brendan the Abbot)

Living with time

The year is the symbol of eternity, for it continually turns round on itself and never comes to rest . . . Christ treats our former life as a thing of the past, and gives us the beginning of a new life . . . according to the pattern of his own death and resurrection.

A reading from a paschal homily of an ancient author, *The Divine Office II*, 509

To see the centrality of the symbol of light as common to both incarnation and resurrection is to see how insepar- able are the Christmas and Easter mysteries. Together they constitute the framework of God's activity in and beyond time, as they form the heart of Christian faith and hope. Without Easter Christmas has no point; with- out Christmas Easter has no meaning . . . The gospel of incarnation and resurrection is not the answer to a set of questions. It is a persistent and defiant light . . .

Kenneth Leech, writing in *The Independent*, 20 December 1992

Living with uncertainty

Without the condition of precariousness as its foundation, religious life dies. How could we remain contemplative in a house with too much certainty?

Fr Christian de Chergé, abbot of the Cistercian community in North Africa, martyred in Algeria, 1996

A religious society must be rickety . . . It must be depend- ent simply upon God for deliverance out of all trouble. The moment a community ceases to be rickety it ceases to be dependent on God.

Fr R. M. Benson SSJE, founder of the Cowley Fathers

Living on the edge is an uncertain business,
the thin edge of the wedge,
a promise not quite honoured,
a shakily held pledge.

Paul Groves, 'Anglo-Welsh', *Landscapes on the Edges: Poems
of the Wye Valley and Welsh Border*, eds Margot Miller and Sue
Sharpe (Ross-on-Wye: Fineleaf, 2010), 27

Living with promise

The threshold has an otherworldy quality to it because
it is neither and not yet, and yet in this suspension the
stage is being set for what is to come – the crop is being
planted so to speak. Only later on do we recognise what
has come to birth.

Thresholds are like those growth knobs on tree limbs:
signs of how far it grew before it accepted an invitation
to grow even more.

Sr Renée Branigan OSB, in a personal letter. (Sr Renée is a
Benedictine sister at the Sacred Heart Monastery, Richardton,
North Dakota)

Living with death and life

I think that the retrieval of a tradition of *defeat* becomes
in itself an affirmation of what is *not defeated* . . . What's
not defeated, what we can't escape from, roots itself in us
whether we like it or not, because it is the landscape of an
identity which we don't understand or master.

Rowan Williams, 'Shaping Holy Lives', in *The Oblate Life*, ed.
Gervase Holdaway OSB (Norwich: Canterbury Press, 2008)

The resurrection is a sign that, even in death, the border is still, contrary to our expectations, open . . . We approach the border, then, with a mixture of faith and uncertainty . . . We do not like coming to the edge of our sphere of control. We do not like the fact that death and new life are all mixed up together here.

L. William Countryman, *Living on the Border of the Holy: The Human Priesthood and the Church* (Harrisburg, PA: Morehouse Publishing, 1978), 79

A Border Anthology

Just as in the art of good conversation it is vital to take time, to listen to the other, to respect their voice and not to intrude, so in this dialogue with the landscape I have to remember that it is essential to do the same – and from the poets I have learnt that the process should be seen as one of unveiling, decoding.

A number of poets and artists who have been inspired by this border landscape have helped me to see it and to listen to it. I am extremely grateful to them for allowing me to reproduce a selection of their work here. It forms a most important part of this book. They have also been ready to introduce themselves and speak of their connection with this area.

Along the Wye

On a glorious summer day
this border country rolls out
in a carpet of green turf,
the fertile result
of a blood-soaked history.
A place where armies marched,
kings were made and broken;
it was not peaceful
as it seems now.

Cistercians nestled their abbeys
among these verdant hills,
built their common life
around prayer-soaked emptiness,
the cloisters at their heart.
Now, though they point east
from darkness to light,
in their skeletal remains
only the wind chants the hours.

Border lands often murmur
of what was and might have been.
Like the Welsh it leads to,
this landscape sings.
God draws back the veil
to make a Golden Valley
between the Black Mountains,
a place teeming with the life
of presence and past.

Bonnie Thurston

Another Welsh Landscape

To live in Wales is to be conscious
Of dissension.
Here we eat paradox for bread,
Share the arteries to everywhere
That stifle circulation;
Nurse a history lost,
A landscape burned in anger.
The valleys echo words
But they send nothing back the same.

The past is a wound.
Wales is sick to death
Of others' pride,
The endured pomp and tramp
Of Roman, Saxon, Norman, Saxon:
The moronic rhythm
That undermined the song,
Tore a tongue out at its root.

But there are relics real to faith;
Potency is here,
Tucked beyond
All the decayed winding-gear
Of the heart.
That howl you hear is birth;
The streaming viscera are placental.

Sometimes the rain lifts;
With the wind in the right quarter
You may catch
An old song making new.

Michael Woodward

Old Song

Birdsong outside my window
recalls tremblings of water.

I lay along
deep in ferns by the stream's edge;
only the bee's hum
and the labyrinthine murmurings
entered my mind.

Birdsong and water bear away grief.
I walked home through the mountain mist
calling your name.

Frances Horowitz

The Promised Land
(for Esther)

A tramp through bog and tussocks,
fog, tormenting rain
was not to view the citadels
imperial in golden power.
   It was to see
   the holy mountain*
one more time,
a far cry from the dark
   abandoned pit,
    that clanking winch,
     the drop.

Was it the blood that called
to the hill's cleft side,
the very blood the chapel
preachers hailed in song
   and wrathful thunder?
   The self-same
now throbs within him at the bidding
of a glad heart released
   where sight and touch
     are one.

An estate of the soul: he may watch
the clouds upon Craig Serrerthin†
moving in heedless clarity
obliterate the blackness of the past.
   A harsh gust
   of Welsh weather
beats up the deserted vale
and whirls him back to home –
   purged in a blessing
   from a world he'd feared
     too long.

Glen Cavaliero

---

*A reference to Skirrid Fawr, with its distinctive scarred slope, which tradition says was caused by a landslide at the third hour of Christ's crucifixion.
†A variation on the Welsh for Hill of Seraphim.

Norman Churches, Herefordshire

Escaping turbulent Oxford
I used to bike to Iffley,
sit in the shadows
of that Norman church
and breathe easier.
I did not know
what drew me,
only that it soothed,
calmed, centered.

Thirty years later
I glimpsed the why
here, in these churches
built of local stone,
churches that seem
to rise from earth
without human help
as naturally as hedgerows
and as full of life.

Their square simplicity
is softened
by arch and apse.
No ornate fan vaulting
draws the eye upward.
Homey dog-toothed arches
tie walls firmly to floor,
make the place solid,
embracing, permanent.

Unpretentious churches
house a practical
life of spirit.
No lace cuffs ever offered
or incense accompanied
the coarse broken bread,
the pewter cup
of rough wine
that tastes of earth.

Unpretentious churches
root the life of this land
in the practice of prayer,
at many crossroads
quietly offer all comers
an invitation to pause,
to rest, to remember
that peace passes
understanding.

Bonnie Thurston

Merthyr Clydawg

Clodock; it sounds rustic, and English.
Clydawg; the lost Welsh is back. He seems
an off-beat martyr, killed for love,
out hunting, by a jealous rival; yet,
a prince who led in battle and prayer,
his story has a spice of miracle. Oxen
(helped by a broken yoke) refused
to drag his body over the ford, insisted
that here should be his burial-place.

In the church, the gallery's music-table
might be straight from Hardy. But Latin
on a dug-up stone remembers
'that faithful woman the dear wife
of Guinnda', who centuries back
lived in this place of shifting boundaries,
strife, loss, perpetual haunting, garbled names,
Welshness in the soil's depth,
unacknowledged riches,
uncomprehended power.

Ruth Bidgood

Circle of Stones by John Neilson.

Dry Stone Walls, Wales

Land of moving light in open fields,
of dark, mysterious valleys,
like the saint's expansive holiness
unable to fit its inhabited space,
the beauty of Wales is so vast
it must be broken into manageable bits.

So the great, windswept mountains,
the green rolling hills,
are marked off by walls,
flat plates of gray stone,
jigsaw of pieces fit lovingly together
by a practiced hand, and artist's eye.

Some, like those up Offa's Dyke, are sharp,
wear only the lichen of a century or so.
Others, in narrow, secret lanes
winding down from old Penalt church,
are immensely old, rounded green with moss
as if earth reaches up to claim her own.

But the sturdiest walls are unseen,
like the cherubim's flaming sword
protect the secret of the makers in stone,
their connection to the Keeper of wanderers,
the Keeper of all lost things,
the meticulous care of that keeping.

Bonnie Thurston

Stone

Arcadia was never here.
Ice-needles tortured the thin soil,
spring snow lay long by the north wall,
yet the peat-fire had a summer heart.
Waves of life receding left
jetsam of stone – grey megaliths
half-sunk in tussocky grass now
but still processional on the ridge above,
leading into a mystery:
in a cranny of the valley, a ring of stones
that sheltered a hearth once; a roofless hut
of later years, perched high upstream
under the shadow of cairned hills.
The rushes cut each autumn
to mend the thatch, one year
were cut no more; over the centuries
the path was lost. Only stone lasts here.
Stone proclaims life, affirms a future
by virtue of so many pasts,
yet baffles questioning. As I touch walls
warm in the sun today, and feel
so many summers gentle to my hand
and yet withheld, I would crush stone
in my fist, if I could, till truth's milk ran.

Ruth Bidgood

Finding a Sheep's Skull

Sudden shock of bone
at the path's edge,
like a larger mushroom
almost hidden by leaves.

I handle the skull gently
shaking out earth and spiders.
Loose teeth chock in the jaw:
it smells of nothing.

I hold it up to sunlight,
a grey-green translucent shell.
Light pours in
    like water
through blades and wafers of bone.
    In secret caves
filaments of skull hang down;
frost and rain have worked
    to shredded lace.

The seasons waste its symmetry.
    It is a cathedral
echoing spring; in its decay
    plainsong of lamb
    and field and sun
inhabits bone.

The shallow cranium
fits in my palm.

– for speculative children
I bring it home.

Frances Horowitz

Green Man

I never met a Green Man
until I stumbled upon him
in Welsh border country.
Then I found him
in every church:
a leafy mask,
a grinning Pan
smirking fertility
in a dusty corner;
or a male head
looking slightly surprised
disgorging vegetation
down a pillar,
over a door frame;
or the hint of a face
furtive behind leaves,
Adam hiding among the trees.

Old as God's third day
and every bit as good,
you flourished
long before the church
grafted you in.
Now, though we try
to tame you, name you
in guide books
and art history,
you burst forth
make even stone live,
turn it to bread
that feeds my hunger
for irrepressible reality.
Root it deep within us,
this healing wholeness,
this wild profusion of life.

Bonnie Thurston

The Cwm of Peace
(for Victor and Esther)

Standing here
Above the plunged scar
Worried out by water,
Nature's sharpest knife,
I feel like a maker
And something fashioned, too;
Another carving, incomplete.

Below,
The loud poured out torrent
Crashing on to granite
Underwrites the silence.
This is a place to pray.

The house sits
Calm as a buddha;
Two shells seamed in to one.
In the cool garden
A hearth's peace pitches its tent
Beneath the blackbirds
Jugging out their psalms.

In this place
Clean of human sound
You can trace the Cwm's silver thread
Along the sheer drop,
Through the stand of hazels
Switching your cheek;
Treading a slow, careful path
Towards the hill's heart.

Michael Woodward

Your Garden – 'One Good Place'
(for Esther)

Was it a wind,
ahead, held back
by a cluster of trees
from your sunny lawn,
your tall anemones?

From stone to slippery stone
I followed you down
until we could witness
that long white water
moving, motionless.

Such a deep cut!
Time wearing down
the land and cleaning
the hidden rock,
letting water go

from sunshine to darkness,
then making it fall
further, changed,
for a spell, from see-through
to wind-voiced brilliance.

How smoothly it bends
on the rim above,
how silently winds
around slabs below
as if innocent of this:

the free fall
that holds, for a spell,
our bodies breathless,
filled a moment
with air-bright water.

Uphill, they met:
two streams, each
a flow out of darkness,
winding on each other
like voices singing.

They've worn a circle
in the high bank –
a potter's thumb
resisting the spin
making space open.

Too fast to move on,
the waters spiral.
We watch some leaves
buoyant but yellow,
not yet drowning.

From the pool's edge,
clear water seeps
secretly among pebbles.
Two dippers flit.
As fish did, once.

Today, polluted,
the water's lifeless,
except for its own
lapses, its own
falls and stagnations.

These are its music,
its almost human
chanting, its almost
human leap
into thin air.

But this is a small
ordinary stream,
no more than rain
on a part of its journey
from sea to sea.

Not a human metaphor.
A secret elegance
in the ways of matter.
Whatever it is
heart-breaking, holding.

Glimpses. A touch
through eye or ear
of something Other.
Clench before it – terror.
Open in it – oneness.

I recall you turning
away, to your garden,
the task practical –
a new place for compost,
a new place for burning –

while the two streams,
their various voices,
hold as in a bowl
your open rooms
(a rush of stillness)

and the slumped side
of Holy Mountain
utters its cry
of astonished silence.
Mourning. Praising.

Anne Cluysenaar

About the Poets

Ruth Bidgood

With a north Welsh father who worked in South Wales, and a West Country mother, and myself born and bred in South Wales but having for many years now returned from a long spell out of Wales to live in mid-Wales, I feel very much a 'borderer'.

As a poet, I distrust certainties, and feel more at home with unknowing – with what I have called 'the mystery that complements precision'.

I describe myself as 'Content for long now with living / in shade, fertile uncertainty, accepting / mystery'.

'Merthyr Clydawg' first appeared in *Singing to Wolves* (Bridgend: Seren Books, 2000) and was reprinted in *Symbols of Plenty* (Norwich: Canterbury Press, 2006).

'Stone' is taken from the collection *The Given Time*,

1972, and appears in *New and Selected Poems* (Bridgend: Seren Books, 2004). Quoted with permission.

Glen Cavaliero

Glen Cavaliero is a Fellow of the Royal Society of Literature and the author of seven collections of poems. He has a particular love for the Anglo-Welsh border country, especially for the Black Mountains and the upper Wye. He lives and teaches in Cambridge, where he is a Fellow Commoner of St Catharine's College.

'The Promised Land' appeared in *The Justice of the Night* (Leyburn, N. Yorkshire: Tartarus Press, 1997). Quoted with permission.

Anne Cluysenaar

Anne Cluysenaar was born in Belgium, brought up in England, Scotland and the South of Ireland, and has for over 20 years lived on the edge of Wentwood Forest in the Welsh Borders. Anne enjoys the sense of liminality, and the titles of her publications sometimes reflect this: for example, her *Timeslips: New and Selected Poems* (Manchester: Carcanet, 1997) and *Migrations* (Blaenau Ffestiniog: Cinnamon Press, 2011).

'Your Garden – "One Good Place"' first appeared in *The Merton Journal*, which explains the subtitle, a phrase of Thomas Merton describing the importance of 'one good place'. Quoted with permission.

Frances Horowitz

Frances cannot speak for herself, except through her poetry, for she died tragically in 1983, at the far too young age of 45. She is buried in Orcop in a grave that looks out towards the Black Mountains. I remember her in the years that she was living with her husband and young son at the mill in Rowlestone. The lines that she wrote about a mythical Welsh figure could be taken as a description of her herself:

> in this valley she walked
>   I remember
> a woman with the smell of wind in her hands
> walking at nightfall in the petals of an early spring . . .

She was strikingly beautiful, striding in freedom, through the lanes and into the hills around her here.

In 'Old Song', she remembers an afternoon at Capel-y-ffin. It is in the anthology *Between the Severn and the Wye*, ed. J. Coppin (Moreton-in-Marsh: Windrush Press, 1993).

'Finding a Sheep's Skull' is from *Snow Light, Water Light* (Newcastle upon Tyne: Bloodaxe Books, 1983).

One year, when we had late snow in April after the early purple orchids had begun to flower (a real crossing of the border of the seasons), she wrote *Rowlstone Haiku*, beautifully produced in a limited edition by the Five Seasons Press in Madley, Hereford, which she dedicated to our family.

I am including the final haiku here as an act of gratitude to a woman whose loss I continue to mourn:

Rich purpled ermine,
orchids bowed in April snow
court rarely convened.

Quoted with permission.

Bonnie Thurston

When Bonnie, an American theologian and poet, first
discovered the border country, which she describes as a
'mystical land', she immediately felt at home, and that
she *belonged*: 'I am a "border person" by geography and
family background.'

For the past decade she has been a regular visitor, with
a circle of close friends and a wide knowledge of both
local people, living and dead, and of the landscape of
the Welsh Borders. The poems that this inspired, including the four poems included here, were first published
by Michael Woodward in *The Heart's Lands* (Abergavenny: Three Peaks Press, 2001), and are now included in
Belonging to Borders (Collegeville, MN: Liturgical Press,
2011). Quoted with permission.

Michael Woodward

Michael lives in Abergavenny, a border town *par excellence*, with Norah and their family. He studied English
at Cambridge, and has travelled in India. Of his first
volume, *A Place to Stand* (Abergavenny: Collective Press,
1995), Rowan Williams said: 'poetry that is dense and
rich, wasting no words'. The two poems included here are
taken from his second collection *Thirst* (Abergavenny:
Three Peaks Press, 2001). Quoted with permission.

Notes on the Illustrations

Landscape at Capel-y-ffin – David Jones (cover and page 6)

Wild Ponies – David Jones (page 72)

In the years spent at Capel with Eric Gill and his family, David Jones (1895–1974) was much influenced by 'the strong hill rhythms and the bright counter rhythms of the water brooks'. It is a constantly changing scene with wild ponies straying over the hill slopes. Often misty, the light comes and goes, and there is the constant background sound of the small brooks which flow over their rock streambeds. Reproduced by permission.

The Shell – Richard Kindersley (page 19 and used throughout)

Threshold stones have been commissioned for the three entrances to Hereford Cathedral, and this is the one to be placed at the main entrance, in the porch of the North door. It is the work of Richard Kindersley, who says of it: 'The shell is of course the symbol of pilgrimage, something that links well with the threshold. We need to discover the way back to being and I have always thought of that as a pilgrimage or journey.' Reproduced by permission.

The Skirrid – Charles MacCarthy (page 74)

Charles MacCarthy moved to Herefordshire 25 years ago and found a landscape whose sheer scale and dramatic impact was very different from anything he had known before. It has taken him time to 'see' this landscape:

> like getting to know people by seeing them in different situations, faces and character eventually become familiar . . . Amongst many other striking landmarks nearby the Skirrid was for me one of the first of these familiar faces, with a form which reminded me of Cézanne's Mont Ste Victoire.

> Sometimes, feeling slightly overwhelmed by the size and brooding presence of these hills and valleys, there was comfort in the familiar outline, one which proclaims a kind of lofty nobility, ancientness, even holiness – the Holy Mountain.

Reproduced by permission.

Capel-y-ffin 'Church Gate and Yews' – Edgar Holloway (page 70)

The place-name Capel-y-ffin means 'place on the boundary, a border place', an apt description since it lies at the foot of the pass between the Llanthony Valley and Hay-on-Wye. His widow says that this small church was painted frequently by Edgar Holloway, who in his later years (he was born in 1914 and died in 2008) returned to the 'tangled, romantic landscape of the Welsh border'. Reproduced by permission.

Circle of Stones – John Neilson (page 97)

Made of red sandstone from a nearby quarry at Michaelchurch Escley, this stands in front of the Monnow Valley Arts Centre, as part of its installation 'Art and Memory'. John Neilson says:

> Each stone carries three or four versions of one place name from near where the stone was quarried – the area known historically as Ewyas Lacy in south-west Herefordshire. The first version (nearest the ground) is the oldest known from written sources, the top is the current one and other versions are between the two. The intention is to suggest both continuity and change in the passing on of language from one generation to the next, and how language is thus a kind of living memorial.

Reproduced by permission.

Notes and References

Introduction

1. Esther de Waal, *Lost in Wonder: Rediscovering the Spiritual Art of Attentiveness* (Norwich: Canterbury Press, 2003; Collegeville, MN: Liturgical Press, 2003).

2. Graham Greene, *The Lawless Roads* (London: Penguin Books, 1939), 19.

3. L. William Countryman, *Forgiven and Forgiving* (Harrisburg, PA: Morehouse Publishing, 1998), 1–2.

4. Paul Hill, 'The Art of David Jones', in *David Jones* (London: Tate Gallery Publications Departments, 1991), 24.

1 The Border Landscape

1. David Jones, *Epoch and Artist* (London: Faber, 1959), 251.

2. R. S. Thomas, *Collected Poems 1945–1990* (London: Phoenix, 1993), 207. Quoted with permission.

3. Bonnie Thurston, *The Heart's Lands* (Abergavenny: Three Peaks Press, 2001), 33. Quoted with permission. The full text of the poem appears on page 90.

4. This is the underlying theme of so much that I have written on the role of order in the Benedictine and Cistercian traditions.

5. *A History of the Benedictine Priory of the Blessed Virgin Mary and St Florent at Monmouth* (Aberystwyth: Cambrian Printers, 2001).

2 Times and Seasons: Crossing Between Light and Dark

1. David Scott, *Sacred Tongues: The Golden Age of Spiritual Writing* (London: SPCK, 2001), 6.

2. There is now a great deal of interesting material on the map. The best short introduction is that of Meryl Jancy, *Mappa Mundi: A Brief Guide* (Hereford: Hereford Cathedral Enterprises, 1995).

3. Leo the Great.

4. See selections from Alexander Carmichael's *Carmina Gadelica* in Esther de Waal, ed., *The Celtic Vision: Prayers, Blessings, Songs, and Invocations from the Gaelic Tradition* (London: Darton, Longman & Todd, 1988; Liguori, MO: Liguori/Triumph, 2001). All quotations from Celtic sources that follow can be found in full in this anthology, which I published in order to make them easily accessible. This is taken from page 151.

5. John Davies, *God at Work: Creation Then and Now – A Practical Exploration* (Norwich: Canterbury Press, 2001), 12.

6. Douglas Dales, *Christ the Golden Blossom: A Treasury of Anglo-Saxon Prayer* (Norwich: Canterbury Press, 2001), 17.

7. Quoted from George Mackay Brown. Source unknown.

8. Brigid Boardman and Philip Jebb, *In a Quiet Garden: Meditations and Prayerful Reflections* (Stratton on the Fosse: Downside Abbey Books, 2000). All of the quotations that I have used in this section are taken from the section on the seasons, 82–88. Quoted with permission.

3 Embracing Life's Changes

1. Robert W. Fynn, *The Lost Bone* (London: Avon Books, 1996), 20–21.

2. The comments were given to Alexander Carmichael as he collected these death blessings. See Esther de Waal, ed., *The Celtic Vision: Prayers, Blessings, Songs, and Invocations from the Gaelic Tradition* (London: Darton, Longman & Todd, 1988; Liguori, MO: Liguori/Triumph, 2001), 112; 133.

3. de Waal, *The Celtic Vision*, 66.

4. Francis Duff, *The Art of Passingover* (New York: Paulist Press, 1988), 153.

5. Walter Brueggemann, *Hopeful Imagination: Prophetic Voices in Exile* (Philadelphia: Fortress Press, 1986).

6. Brueggemann, *Hopeful Imagination*.

Interlude: Crossing over with Saints and Angels

1. D. Gwenallt Jones, 'St. David'. For the full text see pages 39–41 in *Threshold of Light: Prayer and Praises in the Celtic Tradition*, eds A. M. Allchin and Esther de Waal (London: Darton, Longman & Todd, 1986, re-issued, 2004; (US title) *Daily Reading from Prayers and Praises in the Celtic Tradition* (Springfield, IL: Templegate, 1986). © University of Wales Press, permission sought.

2. Ruth Bidgood, *Singing to Wolves* (Bridgend: Seren Books, 2000), 29. Quoted with permission.

3. Ruth Bidgood, *Selected Poems* (Bridgend: Seren Books, 1992), 34. Quoted with permission.

4 Connecting Inner and Outer

1. L. William Countryman, *Living on the Border of the Holy: The Human Priesthood and the Church* (Harrisburg, PA: Morehouse Publishing, 1999).

2. Mick Hales, *Monastic Gardens* (New York: Stewart, Tabori & Chang, 2000), chap. 1, 'The Cloister Garth', 14–30.

3. John Dunne, *The House of Wisdom* (London: SCM Press, 1985).

4. The art of conversation is not only gentler but it is an art that can be learnt. I am grateful to William Countryman for clarification on this small but important point. He helped to put my own experience into clearer perspective (Countryman, *Living on the Border of the Holy*, 205, note 27; 204, note 26). *A Vow of Conversation* was published in Basingstoke, England, by the Lamp Press in 1988.

5. Thomas Merton, *Woods, Shore, Desert: A Notebook, May 1968* (Santa Fe: Museum of New Mexico Press, 1982), 48.

5 The Time Between Times

1. John Howard Griffin, *The Hermitage Journals:, A Diary Kept While Working on the Biography of Thomas Merton* (ed. Conger Beasley Jr; Garden City, NY: Image Books, 1983), 49.

2. Howard Griffin, *The Hermitage Journals*, 1.

3. Howard Griffin, *The Hermitage Journals*, 47–48.

4. Howard Griffin, *The Hermitage Journals*, 73.

5. This is taken from an article in *The Guardian*, 17 February 2002.

6. Mary Morrison, *Let Evening Come: Reflections on Aging* (New York: Doubleday, 1998), 139.

7. These are unpublished poems by Bonnie Thurston and I am grateful to her for allowing me to include them here.

8. Antjie Krog, *Country of My Skull* (Johannesburg, South Africa: Random House, 1998), 99.

9. Wilhelm Verwoerd, *My Winds of Change* (Randburg, South Africa: Ravan Press, 1997).

10. Douglas Dales, *Glory: The Spiritual Theology of Michael Ramsey* (Norwich: Canterbury Press, 2003). The quotations given in this paragraph come successively from pages 46, 15, and 5.

11. Johnston McMaster, 'Celtic Resources for a Peace Process', in *Celtic Threads: Exploring the Wisdom of Our Heritage*, ed. Padraigin Clancy (Dublin: Veritas, 1999), 96–98.

12. This is taken from an article written for *Benedictine*

LIVING ON THE BORDER

Bridge: The Journal of the Sisters of St Benedict (Madison, WI: Advent, 2000). In 1992, the Roman Catholic Sisters of St Benedict of Madison, Wisconsin, began a visionary process that has led to a new ecumenical monastic community following the Rule of St Benedict.

13. Jonathan Sacks, *The Dignity of Difference: How to Avoid the Clash of Civilizations* (London: The Continuum Publishing Group, 2003).

14. I am quoting here from a review article by John Habgood that appeared in *Church Times*.

15. See William Johnston, *Mirror of the Mind* (London: Collins Fount, 1981), 10–11, 14.

16. See John W. Kiser, *The Monks of Tibhirine: Faith, Love, and Terror in Algeria* (New York: St Martin's Press, 2002).

17. See Esther de Waal, *Living with Contradiction: An Introduction to Benedictine Spirituality* (Norwich: Canterbury Press, 1997; Harrisburg, PA: Morehouse Publishing, 1997).

18. Sr Jennifer Dines, *A Touch of Flame: An Anthology of Contemporary Christian Poetry*, comp. Jenny Robertson (London: Lion Paperbacks, 1989), 25.

19. I have gained much from reading Margaret Wheatley, *Leadership and the New Science: Discovering Order in a Chaotic World* (San Francisco: Bennett-Koehler Publishing, 1999), 28.

Afterword

1. See Millichap Peace Fund tape of talk 'From Certainty to Uncertainty: From Dogma to Dialogue', given in Hereford Cathedral on 13 September 2001.

2. Here I make mention of one book among many: John Inge, *A Christian Theology of Place* (Aldershot: Ashgate, 2003, reprinted 2007).

3. I have taken short extracts from three poems. 'Aspects of Stone' comes from the sequence 'The Land', which first appeared in *The Fluent Moment* (Bridgend: Seren Books, 2004), 46, and was included in Ruth Bidgood, *Symbols of Plenty* (Norwich: Canter-

bury Press, 2006), 31. The phrase 'a language half-recognised' is to be found in 'The Well' in *Time Being* (Bridgend: Seren Books, 2009), 40, and the final quotation is from 'Kindred', *New and Selected Poems* (Bridgend: Seren Books, 2004), 215.

4. Charles MacCarthy, 'Fields of Colour': Recent paintings at Piers Feetham Gallery, London, April 2010, expanded in a personal letter.

5. This is taken from her poem 'Walking through Woods'. It is included in *Landscapes on the Edges: Poems of the Wye Valley and Welsh Border*, eds Margot Miller and Sue Sharpe (Ross-on-Wye: Fineleaf, 2010), 59.

6. *The Portfolios of Ansel Adams*, ed. John Szarkowski (New York: Little, Brown & Co, 1977).

7. Ron Seitz, *Song for Nobody: A Memory Vision of Thomas Merton* (Liguori, MO: Liguori/Triumph, 1993), 33–34. A number of Merton's photographs are included in my book *A Retreat with Thomas Merton: A Seven-day Spiritual Journey* (Norwich: Canterbury Press, re-issued 2010).

8. H. J. Massingham, *The Wisdom of the Fields* (London: Collins, 1945), 157.

9. Fernando Caruncho, writing in the *Daily Telegraph*, 8 May 2010.

10. *Moon Tiger* (London: Andre Deutsch, 1987), 68.

11. Preached on 2 November 1986.

12. 'Merthyr Clydawg', Bidgood, *Symbols of Plenty*, 45 (see p. 96).

13. D. Gwenallt Jones (1899–1968), 'St David'. I make no apology for quoting from this poem again (see page 41 and its note). It is a poem to which I return again and again. © University of Wales Press, permission sought.

14. Gouache and pencil on paper, 19 x 13 cm, 1925. In possession of the Tate Gallery. I owe some of what I say here to the exhibition catalogue *Cross Purposes* (2010, Mascalls Gallery, Paddock Wood, Kent), 192.

15. 'Pa Beth Yw Dyn?' ('What is Man?'), Chapter IV: 'Shaping Holy Lives', *The Oblate Life*, ed. Gervase Holdaway OSB (Norwich: Canterbury Press, 2008), 155.

16. Quoted in the 'Afterword' by A. M. Allchin, in Bidgood, *Symbols of Plenty*.

17. I have written about what I like to call 'the vital role of our symbolic identity' in *Seeking Life: The Baptismal Invitation of the Rule of St Benedict* (Norwich: Canterbury Press, 2008), 34–42; Collegeville, MN: Liturgical Press).

18. Quotation from Philoxenus, which I have taken from Kilian McDonnell, *The Baptism of Jesus in the Jordan: The Trinitarian and Cosmic Order of Salvation* (Collegeville, MN: Liturgical Press, 1996), 75.

19. *American Benedictine Review*, 57:2, June 2006, 228–29.

20. 14 March 1870.

21. Jonathan Montaldo, *Dialogues and Silence* (London: SPCK, 2002), xi.

Lightning Source UK Ltd.
Milton Keynes UK
UKHW041132121219
355254UK00013B/1615/P

9 781853 119620